Fusion \ˈfyü zhən\ n.:

a merging of diverse, distinct, or separate elements into a unified whole

Trees \ˈtrēz \ n.:

a theme throughout Scripture

by Chad Bird

CONCORDIA PUBLISHING HOUSE • SAINT LOUIS

3558 S. Jefferson Ave., St. Louis, MO 63118–3968
1-800-325-3040 www.cph.org

Written by Chad Bird
Edited by Mark Sengele
Designed by Karol Bergdolt Bailey

This publication may be available in braille, in large print, or on cassette tape for the visually impaired. Please allow 8 to 12 weeks for delivery. Write to the Library for the Blind, 7550 Watson Rd., St. Louis, MO 63119-4409; call toll-free 1-888-215-2455; or visit the Web site: www.blindmission.org.

Your comments and suggestions concerning the material are appreciated. Please write the Editor of Youth Materials, Concordia Publishing House, 3558 S. Jefferson Avenue, St. Louis, MO 63118–3968.

Manufactured in the United States of America

1 2 3 4 5 6 7 8 9 10 14 13 12 11 10 09 08 07 06 05

Table of Contents

INTRODUCTION

About the Fusion Series

Fusion—the merging of diverse, distinct, or separate elements into a unified whole. Fusion is a word that speaks of energy and excitement, whether you are talking about a style of music or a nuclear reaction.

God's Word is filled with fusion. The Old Testament bears many hints of events to come in the New Testament, yet we often miss the connection. The Gospel message of the Savior is seen time and again in the Old Testament. Through this series you will come to connect—fuse—those events and messages for yourself and your participants.

Each study in the Fusion Series gathers stories from Scripture—both Old and New Testaments—around a common theme. Through the study of that theme we pray that you come to a deeper understanding of the Gospel message of Jesus Christ as Lord and Savior.

Fusion—Trees

From the opening pages of the Bible to the end of Revelation, our Lord is there, embracing His creation to such an extent that time and time again He takes even its most simple elements and uses them for extraordinary good. From the trees of Eden's Garden to the burning bush on Sinai; from the staff of Moses to the shoot of Jesse—all the way to the cross, our heavenly Father uses trees to bless His people.

We embrace the simplicity of the tree of the cross because our Lord embraced it. He embraced it with His Word, He filled it with His presence, and He painted it red with His own lifeblood. So we are not ashamed of it. The crosses in our church are not closeted, but held high, for with St. Paul we confess, "Far be it from me to boast except in the cross of our Lord Jesus Christ, by which the world has been crucified to me, and I to the world" (Galatians 6:14). So let us thank our God for the tree made sacred by His love, for in that tree is carved the epic of our salvation.

Using These Materials

Fusion Series Bible studies are designed to challenge your participants to develop a deeper knowledge and understanding of Scripture. These studies are designed to work for a large-group presentation or small-group Bible study. While there are six sessions outlined in the book, we have not suggested time limits for each section of the lesson. The level of participant interest, discussion, and further questions will help establish the length of time you spend on each section. This flexibility also allows you to use this material for more than six one-hour sessions. You can easily adapt this material to 12 or more hour-long lessons.

Each session contains reproducible participant pages. These pages may be given to participants as you work through the lesson together in class. As an alternative, you may give copies of these pages to participants in advance of the session so that they may complete their personal study before coming to class.

The leader's materials work through the questions from the participant pages and provide additional commentary and insights for the Bible-class leader. You will want to study these notes as you prepare to lead each session.

It is assumed that the Bible-class leader will have the usual basic equipment and supplies available—pencils or pens for each participant and a chalkboard or its equivalent (white board, overhead transparency projector, or newsprint pad and easel) with corresponding markers or chalk. Encourage the participants to bring their own Bibles. Then they can mark useful passages and make notes to guide their personal Bible study and reference later. Do provide additional Bibles, however, for visitors or participants who do not bring one. The appropriate Participant Pages should be copied in a quantity sufficient for the class.

1

THE TWO TREES IN PARADISE

Prayer

It is truly meet, right, and salutary that we should at all times and in all places give thanks unto Thee, O Lord, holy Father, almighty, everlasting God, who on the tree of the cross didst give salvation unto mankind that, whence death arose, thence Life also might rise again; and that he who by a tree once overcame might likewise by a tree be overcome, through Christ, our Lord. Amen.

(Proper Preface for Lent, *The Lutheran Hymnal,* p. 25)

God the Gardener

What kinds of names or images of God do you most commonly associate with Him? What do these names and images tell you about Him? How do they characterize God?

Does God as a "Gardener" or "Tree-Planter" seem like a foreign idea? Why?

Of all the various images and titles that pop into our heads when we think of God—Father, Creator, Savior, Provider—the one that probably ranks near the end of the list (if it makes the list at all!) is that of Gardener. God, after all, is mighty, wise, all-knowing, all-powerful, all sorts of things. But gardener? Yet there is our Lord, right at the beginning of the biblical story, planting a garden for the highest of His creation, Adam and Eve. "And the LORD God planted a garden in Eden, in the east, and there He put the man whom He had formed" (Genesis 2:8).

The whole world belonged to our first parents; they could go wherever they wished, exploring God's good creation that He fashioned for them to enjoy. Yet He not only gave them all the earth, but He also gave them a specific plot of ground on this earth. A place that must have been stunningly beautiful, more beautiful even than the very good creation around it. Out of love, God the gardener gave them Eden.

How do you picture the Garden of Eden? What do you see in your mind's eye? How does Genesis 2 describe it?

What specific kinds of trees grew in the garden? What do you suppose they looked like?

Does their name affect how you picture them or how artists have depicted them?

We are not told particulars about the various kinds of flora and fauna by which this garden was distinguished. No doubt a single glance at such a place would take our breath away, even when compared with the most lovely of garden paradises today. For in that sacred space all was just as it was meant to be. Nothing was out of place. Although we are unaware of all the elements of the garden that made it one-of-a-kind, what we do know is that trees were there—many kinds of trees. They were planted in the soil of Paradise for man and woman to enjoy. They were there as a delight for the eyes and to provide food for the stomach.

Of all the kinds of trees in Eden, however, two in particular are highlighted: the Tree of Life and the Tree of the Knowledge of Good and Evil. Contrary to what we oftentimes assume, what set these trees apart was not necessarily their appearance. They may very well have looked relatively similar to lots of other trees in Paradise. They had no special sap, no unique bark, not even some mysterious kind of fruit. In essence, that is, in their *very nature*, they were ordinary trees, like the thousands of others created by our heavenly Father to adorn His world.

What *did* set them apart, however, what made them everything *but* ordinary, was the *Word* that God spoke concerning them. It is this divine Word attached to these trees that we will focus on in this study. For what that Word *promised* and what that Word *warned* goes to the very heart of the story of creation, the fall into sin, and the re-creation that has been accomplished by Christ. As we will see, trees are deeply rooted in the account of how sin came into the world and how that sin was atoned for on another kind of tree. And in the end, we will also catch a glimpse of how we in the church are promised access to another tree that grows along the streets of the new Jerusalem above.

The Tree That Lives or the Tree That Gives Life?

What function do names have in the Bible?

Can you think of some examples where the names of places or individuals told you much about them?

What does the Bible mean by the name "Tree of Life"? What are some possible explanations?

Right after Moses describes God's work as a gardener, he relays more details about the Lord's handiwork in Eden: "And out of the ground the LORD God made to spring up every tree that is pleasant to the sight and good for food. The tree of life was in the midst of the garden, and the tree of the knowledge of good and evil" (Genesis 2:9).

Names in the Bible rarely have no meaning attached to them. Frequently, indeed the vast majority of the time, names tell us much about a person, place, or thing. So we need to begin by asking ourselves: What exactly did God mean for us to understand about this tree that He named the "Tree of Life"?

He could have meant simply that this tree was truly alive. Seeming more alive than all the others, it flourished in this holy soil of Eden. Perhaps it bedazzled the eyes with its stupendous leaves, made the mouth water for its luscious fruit, was an all-around top-notch piece of flora. God could have meant that, but the testimony of Scripture does not support such a simplistic explanation.

What God also could have meant by this name—in fact, what He did mean—was not so much that the tree was living or that the tree had some kind of extraordinary life, but that the tree *gave* life to Adam and Eve. To say it more precisely, God gave ongoing life to Adam and Eve through this tree and its fruit. Of all the trees in the garden—all of which were living and lovely—this tree alone was designated as the tree through which God would continue to pour down upon Adam and Eve His gift of life, perfect life, a life free of sin, disease, and death. So, if we were to render the Hebrew a bit more exactly, we would translate this name not as the "Tree of Life" but the "tree that gives life." (See AE, vol. 1, p. 92.)

How do we know this to be true? To get the answer explicitly we'll have to jump a little ahead of the story to what God says as He expels Adam and Eve from Eden after they have sinned. After the Lord clothed His rebellious children in animal skins, He said, "'Behold, the man has become like one of Us in knowing good and evil. Now, lest he reach out his hand and take also of *the tree of life and eat, and live forever*—' therefore the LORD God sent him out from the garden of Eden to work the ground from which he was taken. He drove out the man, and at the east of the garden of Eden He placed the cherubim and a flaming sword that turned every way to guard the way to the tree of life." (Genesis 3:22–24, emphasis added)

Read Genesis 3:22–24. Who is meant by the "Us" in "like one of Us"? What would happen if Adam (or Eve) ate of the Tree of Life? How does that help to shed light on what the name means? How is God's action not a punishment but a blessing? In what kind of state would Adam and Eve have lived forever?

First, note the speaker of these words. He says, "the man has become like *one of Us.*" Who is the "Us"? The same God who spoke similar words in the first chapter of Genesis, "Let Us make man in Our image" (Genesis 1:26). The "Us" in both cases points to the Holy Trinity: the Father, Son, and Holy Spirit. These three divine persons lament that Adam had become like one of them in knowing good and evil. Adam and Eve tried to take that which God had not given. Indeed, to obtain it, they resorted to breaking the very command by which God desired to protect them from falling away from His image!

Next, mark well the action God intends to render impossible by expelling Adam and Eve from the garden: "lest he reach out his hand and take also of the tree of life and eat, and live forever—" Then the Lord breaks off His speech in midsentence. He knows what would happen. There is no need to multiply words. If Adam and Eve, having corrupted themselves, would eat of the Tree of Life, they would live forever *in a state of sin and death*. That is what prompts God to expel them from Eden and post a sword-bearing angel to guard the way to the

Tree of Life. For the fruit of that tree would have had the exact opposite effect upon His children from what God had originally intended.

Although stated in negative terms, this verse from after the fall into sin also informs us about the *positive intent* of the tree before sin entered the world. It was planted by God to be a channel for life. Our first parents would have consumed this tree not merely for food but for something better and more lasting than what you grind between your teeth. God knew that even in this perfect Paradise, His people needed more than a full belly. They needed a food to prepare them for the life to come, the life in heaven with Him. So God lovingly provided this most unusual tree, that by eating its fruit they might partake of that life that they would enjoy with Him forever.

How is it that simple fruit—no matter how pleasing to the palate and lovely to the eye it may be—how is it that this ordinary fruit could give such an extraordinary blessing? The answer is the same answer that one can supply time and time again when, in the Scriptures, God performs a miraculous deed or gives some heavenly gift by means of an ordinary part of creation. It was the Word of God, applied to that tree, pumped into its very sap, that set it apart. When God named it "the Tree of Life," that is what it became. His naming creates what it says. The Word of God was in, with, and under the fruit of that tree. This fruit, included in God's command and combined with His Word, bestowed what the divine Word said it would.

Adam and Eve had no need of forgiveness before they disobeyed. So why did God provide this tree? Did they stand in need of something else? How would this tree have prepared them for a heavenly life?

How might we compare this tree with the Sacraments? How does God's Word affect the tree? How does God's Word affect water, bread, and wine?

One sees here an allusion to the Sacraments of Holy Baptism and Holy Communion. Not that Adam and Eve needed forgiveness before their fall into sin! Of course, where there is no sin there is no need of absolution. However, even where there is no sin, there remains the need for life. It was not named the "tree of forgiveness," but "the Tree of Life." And that is precisely what this "sacramental tree" gave to these citizens of Eden. They would take and eat its fruit so that by means of this eating they might receive into their bodies the life of God, the life that He so graciously wishes to bestow. The fruit bore the Word of God into them so that they not only heard the divine Word, they actually ate it.

How important this truth is for our confession of how God works in this world! Even before sin polluted this good creation, God was working sacramentally. He did not merely speak His Word to Adam. Nor did He tell Eve to stare up into heaven until she felt God warming her heart with life. He did no such thing. Instead, He did what He does now. He changed His Word from something just for the ears to make it something for the eyes, the mouth, indeed, the whole person, body and soul. He made His Word tangible, even edible. And so He still acts in the church today. The saving Word is read, sung, chanted, and preached, but it is also splashed onto the bodies of sinners in the wetness of Baptism to cleanse them, enliven them, and make them God's children. It is joined to the food and drink on the altar so that in these elements we dine on the body and blood of Jesus. As it was in the beginning, is now, and shall be forever. Our God is not ashamed of His creation. Rather, He is highly pleased to use it for the good of His creatures—their good in this life and their everlasting good in the life above.

The Tree of the Knowledge of Good and Evil

Read Genesis 2:15–17. How does God introduce His Word about the Tree of the Knowledge of Good and Evil? How does this positive statement help us to better understand the prohibition that follows?

Of the two trees explicitly noted in the account of creation, the second gets more press. And because of the kind of attention the Tree of the

Knowledge of Good and Evil receives, and because of the unhappy outcome of mankind's dealings with its fruit, this tree ends up getting a bad rap. We tend to think simplistically: the "Tree of Life" was good, but the "Tree of the Knowledge of Good and Evil" was bad. We suppose the former was akin to medicine and the latter to poison. Artwork has frequently fallen into this same error, depicting the tree with a skeleton shape or making it look like it belonged more in a dark horror film than a perfect Paradise.

Because we tend to think so negatively of the Tree of the Knowledge of Good and Evil, we suppose that Adam and Eve were to keep their distance from it, not even to go in its general vicinity, lest it reach out like a giant Venus flytrap to snatch them up and devour them! Such a caricature, however, is just that, a misrepresentation. It misses the wholly positive intent of this tree. As we will see, what God meant for people's good turned out for their harm, but through no fault of the tree itself. The blame is to be laid entirely at the feet of the serpentine Satan and the deceived people who abused it. As happens so often still today in our sinful world, the gifts of God are misused and twisted into the reverse of what our Lord created them to be.

As noted above, the Tree of the Knowledge of Good and Evil is first mentioned in Genesis 2:9, in connection with the Tree of Life. Both trees were located in the midst of the Garden of Eden. The Tree of the Knowledge of Good and Evil is mentioned next in connection with the divine Word attached to it. "The Lord God took the man and put him in the garden of Eden to work it and keep it. And the Lord God commanded the man, saying, 'You may surely eat of every tree of the garden, but of the tree of the knowledge of good and evil you shall not eat, for in the day that you eat of it you shall surely die" (Genesis 2:15–17).

When the Lord told Adam and Eve "you shall not eat," how would they have heard these words—with regret, joy, or something else? How would their reaction compare to our reaction to the Lord's various prohibitions?

What was the purpose of the Lord's Word concerning this tree? What prompted them?

The divine Word spoken about this tree is, of course, stated in the negative: "you shall not eat." But we must not rip this one statement out of context, either the context of the verse itself or the context in which it was spoken. First notice that God initially says, "You may surely eat of every tree of the garden." God is demonstrating His overabundant provision of food. The Hebrew way of stating something emphatically is to say a similar form of the verb twice in a row. So, here, God says to Adam and Eve something like this: "You may *eatingly eat* of every tree of the garden." Eat, and eat, then eat some more! There were no bad apples, no poisonous fruits, none of those red-colored berries that all moms and dads warn their children to avoid. Hunger and starvation were not even part of Adam and Eve's vocabulary. Thus, of all the trees in the garden, only one was to be avoided at mealtime. All the rest they could dine on to their stomachs' content.

Second, one must heed the context in which this command was given. When we hear negative commands—prohibitions—we almost always hear these as some law designed to make sure we don't have fun, don't have pleasure, don't have all those things we think we really need. So our ears and hearts—sinful as they are—tend to hear the words to our first parents, "you shall not eat," in the same way that children hear the prohibitions "you shall not climb that tree," "you shall not eat that chocolate chip cookie before dinner," or "you shall not go outside to play until you have finished all your homework." But that is hardly the way Adam and Eve would have heard this prohibition (if they even would have called it that). It was simply the verbalization of God's will. He was telling His beloved children not only what He desired, but what was best for them. It was a good Word, a beloved command. Just as God commanded them, "Be fruitful and multiply" (Genesis 1:28), so He told them, "You shall not eat." Both commands would have been heard by holy ears, understood by holy hearts, and fulfilled in holy lives by our sinless parents. They delighted to keep these divine words, doing what He commanded and avoiding what He forbade, but in both cases delighting in God's will and walking in His ways to the glory of His holy name. Therefore, God was not holding out on Adam and Eve. He was not depriving them of something, but actually giving them something good. That something good was a tree that was bound up with His Word. The Tree of the Knowledge of Good and Evil was thus a Tree of the Divine Word.

There was, of course, a penalty attached to this tree: "for in the day that you eat of it you shall surely die." As in the positive command above, so here the Lord uses an emphatic verb: "you shall 'dyingly die,'" as the Hebrew puts it. The Lord is clear. His Word is sure. He does not hide the danger of not living by His Word. To cling to that Word is to live, but to rebel against that Word is to die. There is no middle state. But as before, this Word is a good Word, a Word that is given to this man and woman, that by heeding it, they may avoid that what it warns against. It is a good command, such as when a father says to his son, "Don't play in the street or a car will run over you," or "Don't play with that electrical socket or you may be electrocuted." These are words spoken out of love and concern, not hatred or in a desire to withhold something useful or needful. They state what is true, objective, unchanging.

What about this tree's intimate connection to the Word of God makes it a source of praise rather than dislike? What might Adam and Eve have discussed when they talked about this tree?

The Tree of the Knowledge of Good and Evil is therefore very similar to the Tree of Life. It is a tree whose identity is entirely determined by the divine Word spoken about it and into it. The Tree of the Knowledge of Good and Evil was not, in its very nature, a deadly tree with poisonous fruit. As Eve herself will later observe, on the surface its fruit was good for food and a delight to the eyes (Genesis 3:6). What distinguished it from all other trees was that, concerning it alone, God had said, "you shall not eat." Had God spoken these same words about the cherry tree, pecan tree, or peach tree, then those trees would have had the same threat of death attached to them. Or, to put it more positively, then those trees would have had the same divine Word attached to them, which Word would have invited and encouraged faith in God's goodness.

When Martin Luther spoke about the Tree of the Knowledge of Good and Evil, he envisioned it in this positive light.

> *So, then, this tree of the knowledge of good and evil, or the place where trees of this kind were planted in large number, would have been the church at which Adam, together with his descendants, would have gathered on the Sabbath day. And after refreshing themselves from the tree of life he would have praised God and lauded Him for the dominion over all the creatures on the earth which had been given to mankind. . . . Adam would have extolled the greatest gift, namely, that he, together with his descendants, was created according to the likeness of God. He would have admonished his descendants to live a holy and sinless life, to work faithfully in the garden, to watch it carefully, and to beware with the greatest care of the tree of the knowledge of good and evil. This outward place, ceremonial, word, and worship man would have had; and later on he would have returned to his working and guarding until a predetermined time had been fulfilled, when he would have been translated to heaven with the utmost pleasure. (AE, vol. 1, pp. 105–106)*

This helps us to answer the question you might have asked yourself: Why was the tree named what it was? Why didn't the Lord call it the "Tree of Death" so that it might clearly be differentiated from the Tree of Life? Dr. Luther has given us the answer to that: primarily because it was not planted and designed to be the source of death, but of life—the life of faith, of liturgy, prayer, preaching, singing, and praising the heavenly Father, who gave them this Divine Word Tree. Under its branches was the church of Adam and Eve. You might still wonder: why was it named the Tree of the Knowledge of Good and Evil? To answer that question, we must move on to Genesis 3, to the saddest story recorded in the annals of human history.

The Darkest Day

Read Genesis 3:1–5. Compare these verses with Revelation 12:9 and 20:2–3. Who really is this serpent?

Read Genesis 2:16 and compare it with the devil's words in Genesis 3:1. What is the serpent doing to the divine Word? In what similar ways does Satan still work in the world today? What kind of picture does Satan paint of God?

We don't know what day it was when Satan came slithering into the holy garden camouflaged as a snake. Many of the church fathers suspected it was on the first day of the man and woman's creation (i.e., Friday); Luther suspected it was the next day. No one really knows, but given Satan's hunger for evil, most suspect that the fallen angel didn't wait long to launch his attack. Even though externally his temptation revolves around a tree and its fruit, the battle really concerns the Word the Lord pronounced about the tree.

We are first informed of the shrewdness of the "snake": "Now the serpent was more crafty than any other beast of the field that the LORD God had made" (Genesis 3:1a). This serpent is no mere reptile, of course, but "the great dragon . . . that ancient serpent, who is called the devil and Satan, the deceiver of the whole world" (Revelation 12:9). For whatever reason, he chose this animal for his disguise. Then he chose his desired victim, Eve, and moved in for the kill. It was to be a war of words.

> *He said to the woman, "Did God actually say, 'You shall not eat of any tree in the garden'?" And the woman said to the serpent, "We may eat of the fruit of the trees in the garden, but God said, 'You shall not eat of the fruit of the tree that is in the midst of the garden, neither shall you touch it, lest you die.'" But the serpent said to the woman, "You will not surely die. For God knows that when you eat of it your eyes will be opened, and you will be like God, knowing good and evil." (Genesis 3:1b–5)*

Eve's first mistake was to engage in a dialogue with the one who loves to talk people into doing things his way. His rhetorical, persuasive skills eventually overcome those who try to engage him on his own terms. The only defense is to quote God's Word, to let it do all the talking. Eve is taken in quickly . . . and lethally.

Compare Genesis 2:16–17 with Eve's quotation of these words in Genesis 3:2–3. Does she quote God word for word? What does she change? Does this impact the meaning?

Compare the initial question Satan asks (Genesis 3:1) with his second statement (3:4–5). How does Satan proceed differently in the second statement? What new argument does the devil use?

The devil goes after Eve by going after the Word of God. First he twists it to mean something completely the opposite of God's original meaning. The Lord had said, "You may surely *eat of every tree* of the garden" (Genesis 2:16, emphasis added), but Satan asks, "Did God actually say, 'You shall *not eat of any tree* in the garden?'" (Genesis 3:1b, emphasis added). He makes it sound as if God is a penny-pinching master, some old Scrooge who is tightfisted with His gifts. Thus the devil first attempts the frontal attack, trying to get Eve to believe that God really does not have her best interests in mind, but is acting purely out of meanness.

Eve responds by quoting the commandment God spoke concerning the tree, but not exactly. She adds to it and alters it. She adds the words, "neither shall you touch it." Some scholars suspect this command was tacked on later by Adam to keep his wife a proper distance from the tree. Maybe Eve came up with it on her own. Either way, it was unnecessary. The concern was not in touching the tree, but eating its fruit. That was the activity forbidden by the divine Word. Next Eve softened—just a touch—the crystal-clear and razor-sharp word of penalty. God warned, "for in the day that you eat of it you shall surely die (literally 'dyingly die')," but Eve says, "lest you die." The difference is subtle, but telling. She drops the temporal element—"in the day"—and she weakens the double verb—"dyingly die"—to a mere "lest you die." Because of the Tempter, Adam's wife was already sliding down the slippery slope that would conclude in the very death about which she had just spoken.

Satan is poised to strike, and strike he does, with suave words artfully spoken to steer Eve's heart further and further from God's Word and her teeth closer and closer to the forbidden fruit. He says, "You will not surely die. For God knows that when you eat of it your eyes will be opened, and you will be like God, knowing good and evil." In other words, "God didn't really mean what He said. He couldn't. What He's really afraid of is you and Adam getting too smart, ending up on His level. He won't kill you. Get real! Just think of what you could have if you took a bite. Why, you could be a goddess yourself and your husband a god! What do you have to lose? Nothing, but—my, oh, my—what you have to gain!"

No further words needed to be spoken. The trap had been set and the bait firmly in place. When the devil was finished with his manipulative speech, he had transformed the tree into an ugly emblem of God's stinginess and selfishness, as well as Adam and Eve's place of opportunity.

Were not Adam and Eve already "like God" since they were made in His image and likeness (Genesis 1:26–27)? So what else was Satan deceiving them into desiring?

Read Genesis 3:6–7. What did Adam and Eve come to "know" immediately after they had eaten the fruit? How does the devil still hold out false hopes when tempting? Give examples.

What was the foundational sin of Adam and Eve—eating from the tree or something else?

Eve, with Adam on her heels, chose to believe the lie of the devil over the truth of God. "So when the woman saw that the tree was good for food, and that it was a delight to the eyes, and that the tree was to be desired to make one wise, she took of its fruit and ate, and she also gave some to her husband who was with her, and he ate. Then the eyes of both were opened, and they knew that they were naked. And they sewed fig leaves together and made themselves loincloths" (Genesis 3:6–7). When all was said and done, it was the serpent, not Adam and Eve, who was licking his lips in triumph.

What does this event tell us about the name of the tree? Why was it called the Tree of the Knowledge of Good *and Evil*?

Now we know why the tree was called the Tree of the Knowledge of Good and Evil. It received that name in light of the effect it produced upon consumption of its fruit. Now Adam and Eve knew not only good—a good God, good gifts, good life—but also evil. They now knew intimately the evil of the devil, the evil of their actions, and the evil of their very own selves, now corrupted by their rebellion against God's will. The fallout from this event is recorded in the remainder of Genesis 3, as well as the rest of the world's history. Every tear, every murder, every broken heart, every grave, every soul descending into hell traces its genesis to this event. Yes, now we know good *and evil*, but the latter dominates in this world intoxicated by sin and death and always thirsty for more.

Read Genesis 3:15, preferably in the King James or New King James version. What promise does God give to Adam and Eve and their descendants? This is the only place in the Old Testament where the pronoun *her* is attached to the word *seed*. What does this already point forward to (Isaiah 7:14)? How does the serpent "bruise" the heel of the woman's seed (offspring; descendant) and how does the woman's seed bruise his (the serpant's) head?

Yet in the midst of this saddest of stories, the light of hope shines. In the form of prophecy, God speaks to the devil, but, with the same words, foretells the coming of One who will undo the works of Satan: "I will put enmity between you and the woman, and between your seed and her Seed; He shall bruise your head, and you shall bruise His heel" (Genesis 3:15 NKJV). This is the only place in the Old Testament where the feminine pronoun *her* is attached to the masculine word *seed*. The promise of "her seed" would strike the Hebrew ear as oddly as "her sperm" would an English speaker. As will be made clearer in later prophecies (e.g., Isaiah 7:14), as well as in its fulfillment, it indicates the birth of One without a human father, without "*his* Seed." Thus the virgin birth is already foreshadowed.

This virgin-born Son will be at odds with the devil, their animosity so intense that it will result in a final showdown in which the Seed "bruises" the head of the serpent while the serpent "bruises" the heel of the Seed. This twofold bruising took place outside Jerusalem as the promised One hung suspended upon—of all things!—a tree, the tree of the cross. As a snake strikes at the heel to inject his poison, and thus "bruises" the heel, so Satan struck out at Jesus. Satan filled Him with the venom of death. In this very death, however, was the death of the devil, the death of his power and tyranny over all fallen Adams and Eves. For when he sank his hellish fangs into the flesh of the new Adam, Jesus pushed with all His might upon the head of that satanic reptile, smashing his skull.

The venom of death had only temporary power over the Son of God. Three days later, while the serpent still lay crushed in defeat, his head bruised beneath the heel of the Seed of the woman, our Savior stood upon His feet, alive again. Death could not hold Him. The venom of the serpent had done its best, but its best was not enough. Victory came when Christ left the tomb, the blood of the snake still on His divine heel.

Read the following Preface, chanted or spoken during the season of Lent: "[We give thanks to God] who on the tree of the cross didst give salvation unto mankind that, whence death arose, thence Life also might rise again; and that he who by a tree once overcame might likewise by a tree be overcome, through Christ, our Lord" (*TLH,* p. 25). How do these words link the tree in Eden to the tree of the cross?

During the season of Lent, the church hears this Proper Preface in the liturgy of the Holy Communion: [We give thanks to God] "who on the tree of the cross didst give salvation unto mankind that, whence death arose, thence Life also might rise again; and that he who by a tree once overcame might likewise by a tree be overcome, through Christ, our Lord" (*TLH,* p. 25). On the tree of the cross, God gave us dead sinners life again. As sin entered the world by the Tree of the Knowledge of Good and Evil, so by the tree of crucifixion forgiveness, life, and salvation came into this world. The word that Adam and Eve disobeyed was obeyed by our Lord. He was "obedient to the point of death, even death on a cross" (Philippians 2:8). As Satan once overcame by a tree, so he likewise was overcome by a tree. The cross became the Tree of the Knowledge of Good and Good and even more Good. In the death of Christ we see the goodness and loving-kindness of our God. There He gives us more than we lost in Adam. There we are reconciled to Him. In that bloody death, Satan is defeated and we are made the children of God once more.

Trees of Life

In two sections of Scripture, both of which describe to us the new Jerusalem, prophets speak of groups of trees that are new and better Trees of Life for the children of God.

Read Ezekiel 47:1–12. In this chapter the prophet is describing a temple he sees in a vision. This temple is symbolic of the holy Christian church. What does Ezekiel see flowing from underneath this temple? How is this river described?

The prophet Ezekiel lived in the sixth century B.C. He preached to the Israelites who had been exiled to Babylon. As they suffered the various afflictions that accompanied their life in a foreign land, Ezekiel often foretold the coming of the Messiah, who would restore them to peace and life in the presence of God. At the end of his book (chapters 40–48), he records an expansive, detailed description of a vision he had of the new Jerusalem and the temple located therein. This vision is of the one, holy, Christian, and apostolic church, "built on the foundation of the apostles and prophets, Christ

Jesus Himself being the cornerstone, in whom the whole structure, being joined together, grows into a holy temple in the Lord" (Ephesians 2:20–21).

Central to the city is the temple, the location of the Most Holy Place, where God had graciously placed Himself for the sake of His people. There is the throne room of the King of kings. As Ezekiel approaches this temple, he beholds a river flowing out from under the side of it (Ezekiel 47:1–12). He walks in the water for a while as it flows down toward the Dead Sea, until the current becomes too deep. When the waters reach that sea, famous for its unbelievably high salt content, the waters from the temple river remove the salt. The Dead Sea is actually desalinated! The waters are divine waters, full of the healing power of the presence of God.

This river is clearly intended to remind us of that river that flowed out of Eden (Genesis 2:10). But that is not all that is "Edenlike" about this scene, for "on the banks, on both sides of the river, there will grow all kinds of trees for food. Their leaves will not wither, nor their fruit fail, but they will bear fresh fruit every month, because the water for them flows from the sanctuary. Their fruit will be for food, and their leaves for healing" (Ezekiel 47:12).

Compare Ezekiel's vision with Revelation 21–22. Ezekiel goes to great lengths to describe the temple in his vision, but St. John says there is no temple. What is the "temple" for John (Revelation 21:22)?

Before we explore these trees Ezekiel saw, and their connection to this amazing river, we need to look at the last book of the Bible. Here, St. John reports that he saw something very similar when he had a vision of the new Jerusalem. Beginning a chapter earlier, in Revelation 21, John begins to describe various aspects of the "holy city, new Jerusalem, coming down out of heaven from God" (Revelation 21:2). He describes the appearance and size of the gates, the streets, and the walls of the city. Like Ezekiel, he is very detailed in his portrayal of this celestial place. Unlike Ezekiel, however, who used lots of ink to describe the temple in the city, John notes that he "saw no temple in the city" (Revelation 21:22a). How, you might ask, can John so closely follow Ezekiel, but see no temple in the new Jerusalem? The answer lies in the rest of the verse: "I saw no temple in the city, for its temple is the Lord God the Almighty and the Lamb" (Revelation 21:22). So John *did* see a temple, just not a building, as Ezekiel described it. John saw the reality Himself, the God who was enthroned within the temple!

This identification of God and His Lamb, on the one hand, and the temple on the other, is of the greatest importance in what follows. For John, like Ezekiel, highlights a river in this Jerusalem above. And, like Ezekiel, he sees this river flowing from the temple, although he does not use that exact language. Remember, for John, the temple is not a house of wood and stone and precious metals but the Father and the Son, the Lord God Almighty and the Lamb who takes away the sin of the world. John says, "Then the angel showed me the river of the water of life, bright as crystal, flowing from the throne of God and of the Lamb through the middle of the street of the city; also, on either side of the river, the tree of life with its twelve kinds of fruit, yielding its fruit each month. The leaves of the tree were for the healing of the nations" (Revelation 22:1–2). Thus, for John the "throne of God and of the Lamb" has replaced the temple of Ezekiel. The throne and temple, however, are describing the same thing—the gracious presence of the triune God.

Pay careful attention to how, even though the visionary descriptions of these two messengers of God are not exactly the same, they are very similar.

Compare Ezekiel's description of the river with Revelation 22:1–2. How are these rivers similar? Use the following chart.

VISION	EZEKIEL	JOHN
Source of river	Below the threshold of the temple	From the throne of God and of the Lamb
Where it flows	Through the city to the Dead Sea	Through the middle of the street of the city
What kinds of trees	All kinds of trees	The Tree of Life
Where the trees grow	On the banks, on both sides of the river	On either side of the river
When the trees bear fruit	Every month	Each month
The purpose of their fruit	For food	
The purpose of their leaves	For healing	For the healing of the nations

Both Ezekiel and John portray the new Jerusalem as Paradise regained, a new and better Garden of Eden, where all of us baptized Adams and Eves can live with God in perfection forever. As with the first Eden, this second Eden has a river, trees, and fruit. We are told explicitly what their purpose is: the river that flows from God Himself conveys the life of God, the trees grant life like the Tree of Life, and the fruit of the trees is for food.

Compare the visions of John and Ezekiel with the Garden of Eden. What aspects of the garden and the trees are these prophets drawing upon in their own writing? What does this tell us about heaven and what it will be like? What does the new and better Tree of Life give us that it did not give Adam and Eve?

There are several features of these trees that are different from, or expand upon, the purpose of the Tree of Life in the original Paradise. First of all, Ezekiel describes "all kinds of trees" while John speaks singularly of the "Tree of Life." This is really no great difference. Both are clearly "dipping their brushes" in the colors of Genesis 2–3 to paint a scene that recalls Eden. Since even John speaks of the "Tree of Life" that grows "on either side of the river," he is probably speaking of the plural by using the singular; that is, he is indicating that there are several individual trees that are of what one might call the "genus" of the "Tree of Life." Just as when we say, "The pine tree grows in the mountains," we do not mean *a single* pine tree but the genus "pine tree" grows there, so John says the "Tree of Life" grows "on either side." He means that several individual Trees of Life grow there, not that one giant tree stretches from one side to the other and is rooted in the soil on both banks of the river.

Second, nothing is said in Genesis about how often the Tree of Life produced fruit. Ezekiel, however, indicates that in the new Jerusalem "they will bear fresh fruit every month," and John echoes this, saying that the Tree of Life has "twelve kinds of fruit, yielding its fruit each month." Third, no mention is made of the leaves of the original Tree of Life. But both prophets say that the new and better Tree of Life is significant not only for its fruit, but also for its foliage. Ezekiel simply says, "their leaves are for *healing,"* while John adds, "the leaves of the tree were for the healing *of the nations."*

What importance should we attach to these differences? The primary importance is this: the Trees of Life in the new Jerusalem are superior to the Tree of Life in the original Garden of Eden. Though this everlasting paradise is like the one enjoyed by Adam and Eve, it is better. God has given more to His redeemed people than was lost when the first two people transgressed the Law. We gain more in Christ than we lost in Adam. In the heavenly Garden of Eden we shall be with God forever, partake of the fruit of His trees, be healed by their leaves, and enjoy everlastingly all that God has accomplished for us in His Son. All the sin and death that polluted the world because our first parents ate the fruit of the Tree of the Knowledge of Good and Evil will be eradicated. We will know only good—the good of the Tree that gives life in heaven.

The Tree of Death That Gives Us Life

Jesus said to the thief who was crucified beside Him, "Truly, I say to you, today you will be with Me in Paradise" (Luke 23:43). In Paradise—that is where we shall be as well. Our Lord spoke those words from a tree—the tree of the cross. There, all the guilt of Adam, Eve, you, and all other sinners was placed upon God. On that tree, He Himself bore all our lust, greed, meanness, lies, and murder—all of our sins. As sin arose from a tree, so it was destroyed on a tree. From the Man who hangs on this accursed tree, we eat of the fruit of life, the fruit of forgiveness, the fruit of salvation. His body and blood are the fruit that enters our mouths. He who hangs on the crucifixion tree fills our bodies and souls with the fruit that heals all our woes and fills us with the hope of Paradise.

Closing Prayer

"Blessed are You, O Lord our God, king of all creation, for You have had mercy on us and given Your only-begotten Son that whoever believes in Him should not perish but have eternal life. In Your righteous judgment You condemned the sin of Adam and Eve, who ate the forbidden fruit, and You justly barred them and all their children from the tree of life. Yet, in Your great mercy, You promised salvation by a second Adam, Your Son, Jesus Christ, our Lord, and made His cross a life-giving tree for all who trust in Him. We give You thanks for the redemption You have prepared for us through Jesus Christ. Grant us Your Holy Spirit that we may faithfully eat and drink of the fruits of His cross and receive the blessings of forgiveness, life, and salvation that come to us in His body and blood."

(*Hymnal Supplement 98,* p. 11)

The Two Trees of Paradise

God the Gardener

What kinds of names or images of God do you most commonly associate with Him? What do these names and images tell you about Him? How do they characterize God?

Does God as a "Gardener" or "Tree-Planter" seem like a foreign idea? Why?

How do you picture the Garden of Eden? What do you see in your mind's eye? How does **Genesis 2** describe it?

What specific kinds of trees grew in the garden? What do you suppose they looked like? Does their name affect how you picture them or how artists have depicted them?

The Tree That Lives or the Tree That Gives Life?

What function do names have in the Bible? Can you think of some examples where the names of places or individuals told you much about them?

What does the Bible mean by the name "Tree of Life"? What are some possible explanations?

Read **Genesis 3:22–24**. Who is meant by the "Us" in "like one of Us"? What would happen if Adam (or Eve) ate of the Tree of Life? How does that help to shed light on what the name means? How is God's action not a punishment but a blessing? In what kind of state would Adam and Eve have lived forever?

Adam and Eve had no need of forgiveness before they disobeyed. So why did God provide this tree? Did they stand in need of something else? How would this tree have prepared them for a heavenly life?

How might we compare this tree with the Sacraments? How does God's Word affect the tree? How does God's Word affect water, bread, and wine?

The Tree of the Knowledge of Good and Evil

Read **Genesis 2:15–17.** How does God introduce His Word about the Tree of the Knowledge of Good and Evil? How does this positive statement help us to better understand the prohibition that follows?

When the Lord told Adam and Eve "you shall not eat," how would they have heard these words—with regret, joy, or something else? How would their reaction compare to our reaction to the Lord's various prohibitions?

What was the purpose of the Lord's Word concerning this tree? What prompted them?

What about this tree's intimate connection to the Word of God makes it a source of praise rather than dislike? What might Adam and Eve have discussed when they talked about this tree?

The Darkest Day

Read **Genesis 3:1–5**. Compare these verses with **Revelation 12:9** and **20:2–3**. Who really is this serpent?

Read **Genesis 2:16** and compare it with the devil's words in **Genesis 3:1**. What is the serpent doing to the divine Word? In what similar ways does Satan still work in the world today? What kind of picture does Satan paint of God?

Compare **Genesis 2:16–17** with Eve's quotation of these words in **Genesis 3:2–3**. Does she quote God word for word? What does she change? Does this impact the meaning?

Compare the initial question Satan asks (**Genesis 3:1**) with his second statement (**3:4–5**). How does Satan proceed differently in the second statement? What new argument does the devil use?

Were not Adam and Eve already "like God" since they were made in His image and likeness (**Genesis 1:26–27**)? So what else was Satan deceiving them into desiring?

Read **Genesis 3:6–7**. What did Adam and Eve come to "know" immediately after they had eaten the fruit?
How does the devil still hold out false hopes when tempting? Give examples.

What was the foundational sin of Adam and Eve—eating from the tree or something else?

What does this event tell us about the name of the tree? Why was it called the Tree of the Knowledge of Good *and Evil?*

Read **Genesis 3:15**, preferably in the King James or New King James version. What promise does God give to Adam and Eve and their descendants? This is the only place in the Old Testament where the pronoun *her* is attached to the word *seed.* What does this already point forward to *(Isaiah 7:14)*? How does the serpent "bruise" the heel of the woman's seed (offspring; descendant) and how does the woman's seed bruise his (the serpent's) head?

Read the following Preface, chanted or spoken during the season of Lent: [We give thanks to God] "who on the tree of the cross didst give salvation unto mankind that, whence death arose, thence Life also might rise again; and that he who by a tree once overcame might likewise by a tree be overcome, through Christ, our Lord" (*TLH,* p. 25). How do these words link the tree in Eden to the tree of the cross?

Trees of Life

Read **Ezekiel 47:1–12**. In this chapter the prophet is describing a temple he sees in a vision. This temple is symbolic of the holy Christian church. What does Ezekiel see flowing from underneath this temple? How is this river described?

Compare Ezekiel's vision with **Revelation 21–22**. Ezekiel goes to great lengths to describe the temple in his vision, but St. John says there is no temple. What is the "temple" for John (**Revelation 21:22**)?

Compare Ezekiel's description of the river with **Revelation 22:1–2.** How are these rivers similar? Use the following chart, filling in the blanks.

VISION	EZEKIEL	JOHN
Source of river		
Where it flows		
What kinds of trees		
Where the trees grow		
When the trees bear fruit		
The purpose of their fruit		
The purpose of their leaves		

Compare the visions of John and Ezekiel with the Garden of Eden. What aspects of the garden and the trees are these prophets drawing upon in their own writing? What does this tell us about heaven and what it will be like? What does the new and better Tree of Life give us that it did not give Adam and Eve?

2

The Burning Bush

Prayer

Lord Jesus Christ, Son of the Father, who in loving-kindness came down from heaven to speak to Your servant Moses about Your love for Your people, Israel, grant that we who have been united to Your flesh in Holy Baptism may be kept in Your love until we reach the heavenly fatherland. For You live and reign with the Father and the Holy Spirit, one God, now and forever. Amen.

The God of Revelation

Do most people think that God is near or far from His creation? How do they think He interacts with it, if He does at all? With what do they associate His appearances? How might their view of how God reveals Himself affect their view of Him?

The one and only true God is not an aloof deity. He does not isolate Himself from the world He made, erect a high and holy throne, and look down upon creation from afar. At one time this was a highly popular view of God and His interaction with the world. Many people today still hold this erroneous view. This false doctrine, called Deism, compares God to a watchmaker. The watchmaker carefully crafts a timepiece, using all his wisdom and skill, then winds it up and steps back to watch it tick away. The watchmaker views his creation from a distance, admiring his handiwork, and watching it do what he made it to do. Deism claims that God used all His wisdom, power, and skill to make the heavens and the earth. He produced a good creation. He gave every individual part of this world a place and a function in the whole. Once God was finished, He stepped back to look it over. He was pleased with what He had made. From then on, God has sat high in the heavens, looking down upon creation, letting its seasons run their courses, its people live their lives, and so on. God's "cosmic watch" ticks away, year after year, century after century. Though He looks on, He does not interfere, does not interact with His creation, and certainly does not reveal Himself to the creatures below. He is watching everything from a distance. Such is the false claim of Deism.

The true God is quite the opposite. He is the maker of heaven and earth—and of all things visible and invisible—as we confess in the Nicene Creed. He formed a perfect world, in which everything had its place and function. It was not only "good"; it was "very good." But God did not create this world the way a watchmaker crafts a timepiece. First of all, He made it out of nothing, not preexisting materials. "By faith we understand that the universe was created by the Word of God, so that *what is seen was not made out of things that are visible*," as the author of Hebrews says (11:3, emphasis added). He created *ex nihilo*—"out of nothing." God spoke and creation was. The Word of the Father brought into being what He spoke.

God did not make this world to view it from a heavenly distance. He created this world to interact with it, to be in it, to make Himself known to its inhabitants. From the very beginning, He reveals Himself. Though the modes of revelation vary from place to place and time to time, God is everything but standoffish. Rather, He stands close. He stands ready. As Paul describes Him to the pagan crowds on the famous Areopagus in Athens: "[God] made from one man every nation of mankind to live on all the face of the earth, having determined allotted periods and the boundaries of their dwelling place, that they should seek God, in the hope that they might feel their way toward Him and find Him. *Yet He is actually not far from each one of us*, for 'In Him we live and move and have our being;' as even some of your own poets have said, 'For we are indeed His offspring' " (Acts 17:26–28, emphasis added). Though there are places where we do not expect Him to be, He is nonetheless present. Everywhere His Word is spoken, His baptismal water splashed, His body and blood consumed, there God makes Himself known to those who have ears to hear, bodies to wash, mouths to dine. Thus the Deists are dead wrong. God is not a watchmaker. He is a loving Creator who wishes to be known and believed.

Think of incidents in the Bible when God revealed Himself to people. How did He appear, for example, to Adam and Eve in the garden (Genesis 3:8); to Abraham (Genesis

15:12–21); to the Israelites at Mount Sinai (Exodus 19–20); to Jesus at His Baptism (Matthew 3:13–17)? What is similar and what is different about these incidents?

In the Book of Exodus, there are numerous instances where God reveals Himself. He visibly appears to His people, most notably to Moses. In these cases, He temporarily assumes a created form and speaks to Moses or the Israelites. Some of these divine appearances are quite frightening, such as at Mount Sinai when the Ten Commandments are spoken (Exodus 20). Others, while not as alarming, are still enough to cause considerable fright. After all, it is no man, but *God* who reveals Himself! But the purpose of the vast majority of these revelations is not to make the Israelites quiver with fright, but to speak words of comfort, hope, and redemption to the people God loves. He reveals Himself to affirm His promise to never leave or forsake the church.

Read Colossians 2:9. What does Paul say about where we see the full revelation of God? Why is this so important?

The ultimate revelation of God was in the tiny baby Mary held to her virgin bosom. "For in Him the whole fullness of deity dwells bodily" (Colossians 2:9). He is fully God and fully flesh and blood. In this Son of God and Son of Mary, we see the Father and the Spirit. He reveals all of God. And He who is the ultimate revelation is He who revealed Himself on the cross. In that bloody man, dying an agonizing death on the cross, we see the Lord with perfect clarity, for there we see Him lovingly making the ultimate sacrifice to save us. Yes, He is hidden in such a way that our natural eyes cannot behold Him. But if we see what God says we should see on that crucifixion tree, if we look "through our ears," that is, according to God's Word, then we behold the clearest expression of the glory of God. There is God in flesh and blood, *crucified* flesh and *dripping* blood.

On that most famous tree, God revealed Himself in the profoundest way possible. But God had revealed Himself on a tree earlier as well, or, more precisely, in a little tree, a bush. Into a common bush atop a common mountain, God came down to have a dialogue with a shepherd for whom He had uncommon plans. It is on this bush, the "burning bush" as we usually call it, that we will focus in this study. In the story of the burning bush, we will see what kind of God we have, how He chooses to reveal Himself, and what this teaches us about the greatest revelation of God: the Babe of Bethlehem, born to become the Crucified of Calvary.

The Shepherd Moses

Review the history of Israel from the last few chapters of Genesis to the second chapter of Exodus. How did Jacob and his children end up in Egypt? What happened to them when there—both good and bad? What caused Pharaoh to begin his murderous cleansing? How was Moses rescued? Where did he grow up? How did he end up a refugee?

By the time we get to chapter 3 in the Book of Exodus, quite a bit of the story has already transpired. Exodus is the sequel to Genesis. It continues the account of what happened to the descendants of Jacob in Egypt. As you may recall, once they were settled in this land of pyramids, they began to prosper. For many years, they had political security and protection. Because of the good Joseph had done, Pharaoh looked favorably upon Joseph's family. As Exodus summarily puts it: "The people of Israel were fruitful and increased greatly; they multiplied and grew exceedingly strong, so that the land was filled with them" (Exodus 1:7).

There came a time, however, when a king arose in Egypt who did not know about Joseph and all he had done for Egypt. The large numbers of Israelites deeply troubled him. "What if an enemy nation attacked and the Israelites joined with these foes?" he mused. Egypt wouldn't stand a chance. Something had to be done. Pharaoh first tried enslaving the Israelites and forcing them to hard labor, but they prospered even more. When that failed, he initiated one of history's first recorded cases of ethnic cleansing. He ordered the midwives of the Hebrews to kill every male child as soon as he exited the womb. But the midwives, who feared the King of heaven more than the king of Egypt, refused to keep the murderous order. They slyly let all the children live, male and female. So when that too failed, Pharaoh broadened the law so that every Egyptian was essentially commissioned to be a nationally sanctioned assassin of Israelite baby boys. The tiny infants were to be hurled into the Nile River.

At least one babe escaped this watery grave. His mother hid him for three months, then built a tiny boat out of bulrushes, placed him in it, and set him adrift in the Nile. By the providence of God, he was discovered by the daughter of Pharaoh, who named the foundling Moses. Ironically, the princess hired his own mother as the boy's wet-nurse. Once weaned, he was reared in the royal palace. There he remained for almost four decades, Israelite by blood but Egyptian by adoption. Then one day his life took an apparent turn for the worse. He rescued a fellow Israelite from a beating by killing the Egyptian who was giving it. The next day, when Moses found out that his deed was publicly known and that his own life was thus in danger, he hightailed it to the wilderness of Midian. There he met the family of Reuel (a.k.a. Jethro), married one of his daughters, fathered two sons, and lived the life of a shepherd. For nearly 40 years, up to the age of 80, he resided in this wilderness. Until one day . . .

Here is how Moses himself describes what happened:

> *Moses was keeping the flock of his father-in-law, Jethro, the priest of Midian, and he led his flock to the west side of the wilderness and came to Horeb, the mountain of God. And the angel of the LORD appeared to him in a flame of fire out of the midst of a bush. He looked, and behold, the bush was burning, yet it was not consumed. And Moses said, "I will turn aside to see this great sight, why the bush is not burned." When the LORD saw that he turned aside to see, God called to him out of the bush, "Moses, Moses!" And he said, "Here I am." Then He said, "Do not come near; take your sandals off your feet, for the place on which you are standing is holy ground." And He said, "I am the God of your father, the God of Abraham, the God of Isaac, and the God of Jacob." And Moses hid his face, for he was afraid to look at God. (Exodus 3:1–6)*

The Mountain of God

Read Exodus 3 (especially vv. 1–6). In what vocation was Moses engaged when the Lord appeared to him? What did the Lord call him to do? Compare Exodus 3:1 with Psalm 77:20. How was Moses called from one vocation to a similar vocation? How did the Lord Jesus work in a similar way with Matthew (Matthew 9:9–13) as well as with Peter, Andrew, James, and John (Matthew 4:18–22)? Matthew was called from handling money to handling what kind of treasure? Peter and the other men were called to become what kind of fishermen?

Moses, we are told, was engaged in the duties of his vocation on the day he saw this strange fire. As a shepherd, he was, of course, responsible for protecting the flock as well as leading them to grass and water. Presumably, he led his flock near Horeb because there he supposed he could find nourishment for the animals under his charge. Moses was thus faithfully fulfilling what God called him to do at the exact time God called him to another vocation. Such divine timing is worth noting, for it is also the pattern followed by our Lord Jesus when He called (at least some of) His disciples. Matthew, you will recall, was sitting at his tax-collector's booth when Jesus said, "Follow Me" (Matthew 9:9–13). He was called away from collecting earthly riches to distributing freely the heavenly riches of the Gospel. Peter, Andrew, James, and John were busily taking care of the duties of fishermen (Matthew 4:18–32); they were called from being fishers of fish to being "fishers of men" (Matthew 4:19). We have a similar precedent set with Moses. He was caring for the sheep of his father-in-law when he was called to leave the life of shepherding sheep to be a shepherd of God's people. As the psalmist says, "You led Your people like a flock by the hand of Moses and Aaron" (77:20).

Why is Horeb, or Sinai, called the "mountain of God"? What made it especially *God's* mountain? Compare this terminology with similar phrases elsewhere in the Bible. For instance, fill in "the ______ of God" with the aid of the

following verses: Ezekiel 28:13; Psalm 46:4; 1 Chronicles 6:48. What makes each of these special?

The mountain to which Moses led his sheep is known by two names: Horeb and Sinai. Some scholars opine that Horeb designates a mountain range whereas Sinai is the name of a specific peak. The geography, however, is far from conclusive. Either way, this Horeb, or Sinai, is the same mountain upon which God will later descend in fire, smoke, and thunder (Exodus 20). We'll have occasion later in this study to compare that unforgettable revelation of God with this one at the burning bush.

The peak is referred to by a unique title: the mountain of God. Why such a designation? Some suppose that this mountain must already, at the time of the calling of Moses, have had some special religious significance. Since Jethro, the father-in-law of Moses, was a priest, perhaps it was a sacred mount to him and his family, they argue. But this is sheer conjecture. There is nothing in the biblical witness to support the claim that Sinai, or Horeb, was anything but a common mountain at this time. So why does it have this title? Remember that these events were recorded after the call of Moses, and likely after the giving of the Law. Therefore, at the time Moses wrote, Sinai had become intimately associated with the revelation of God. It is thus designated the "mountain of God" because of what was later to transpire there.

Although all the earth belonged to God, this mountain was special, set apart as divine land. In this way, Horeb shares with many other localities in Scripture the characteristics of sacred space. Beginning with Eden, God chooses certain geographical spots and marks them as his own. Whatever spatial area fills in the blank in the possessive phrase "the _____ of God" becomes holy ground. For instance, there is Eden, "the garden of God" (Ezekiel 28:13); Zion, "the city of God" (Psalm 46:4); and the temple, "the house of God" (1 Chronicles 6:48). Similarly, the country of Canaan that God promised Abraham and his descendants is "holy land" (Psalm 78:54), that is, "the land of God." In all these places, God is uniquely present on behalf of His Old Testament church.

Is sacred space still important in the church? Why or why not?

For Old Testament believers, the temple was the place where they went to be in God's presence, to hear His Word, to receive His gifts. Where does Jesus say our temple is now (John 2:21)? How do we enter this new "temple"?

This has all changed in the New Testament church, though, hasn't it? Geography is no longer of interest to us who live under the new covenant, is it? Yes, it most certainly is! Though the geography has changed and holy spaces have shifted, we are still believers who are deeply rooted in sacred soil. Most important, God still locates Himself in specific places for us. Just as He was found by Israelites at the temple, within the Most Holy Place, so the Son of God is found by us in the temple of His fleshly body (John 1:14; 2:21). This body is the physical reality into which we are baptized. His flesh is the Most Holy Place that we now eat in the Lord's Supper. Believers still travel to the temple to be in the presence of God; that is, they go to the temple of Christ's flesh.

Read Hebrews 12:22–24. What and where is this "Mount Zion"? Note the tense of the verbs: are they past tense or future tense? That is, have we *already come* or *will* we come? How does this section help us to answer the question of the importance of sacred space in the church?

Just as the people of Israel went to Mount Zion, to the holy city, so we, too, go to our Zion, to the church, which is not a reality "somewhere out there" but very much spatially and temporally *here and now*. In whatever space God's Word is preached, upon whatever soil the Lord's Baptism and Communion are given and received, there is His church, the new and better Zion. The author of Hebrews expresses it most beautifully when he says to his Christian readers, "You have come to

Mount Zion and to the city of the living God, the heavenly Jerusalem, and to innumerable angels in festal gathering, and to the assembly of the firstborn who are enrolled in heaven, and to God, the judge of all, and to the spirits of the righteous made perfect, and to Jesus, the mediator of a new covenant, and to the sprinkled blood that speaks a better word than the blood of Abel" (12:22–24). Notice that he does *not* say "you *will* come," but "you *have* come." Those who are in Christ *have come* and *continue to come* onto sacred soil, to the Zion of the church, where angels and men gather round the Word of God and the blood of the covenant.

Therefore, just as Moses encountered God at Horeb, the "mountain of God," so we have been granted our own mountain, our own sacred space. That place of revelation is in the church, the holy ground where God is still at work, speaking to make known His will and His ways to those who are His own.

The *Malach* of Yahweh

Read Exodus 3:2. Who appears to Moses in the burning bush? What do you think of when the word *angel* is spoken? The Hebrew word used here is *malach.* Though it is usually translated as angel, the word simply means "messenger."

When the shepherd Moses showed up at Horeb, the Lord arrived also, or, more specifically, "the angel of the LORD." We read, "And the angel of the LORD appeared to him in a flame of fire out of the midst of a bush" (Exodus 3:2). Your translation likely has "LORD" as it appears here, in all capital letters. This manner of spelling is the usual way in which English translations of the Old Testament distinguish the divine name Yahweh from other Hebrew names or titles that are also usually translated as *Lord,* such as *Adonai* ("my Lord"). So who is this "angel of Yahweh"?

To begin with, one must realize that the Hebrew word for *angel* (*malach* or *malak*) simply means "messenger." The "*malach* of Yahweh" is thus the one who bears a message from the Lord. He is there not to speak his own opinion, but to preach the Word of God, to convey to Moses that which the Lord wants him to hear. You might be thinking, "With such a broad definition, one could apply the Hebrew word *malach* to more than just heavenly beings." That is true. And, indeed, that is just what we find in the Scriptures! For instance, the last of the Minor Prophets is Malachi. This prophet's name is simply *malach* with the first person singular pronoun (*my*) attached to it. Thus, *Malachi* means "My messenger," that is, God's spokesman. The prophet is not an angel, of course, as we usually think of angels. But he does have an angelic calling: he proclaims the words of God that are given him to speak.

Now turn to the last book of the Old Testament—Malachi. The name of this prophet simply means "My malach," that is, "My messenger." Read Malachi 2:7. Most English translations will render the last part of the verse as "he is the messenger of the LORD of hosts." The Hebrew word is again *malach.* To what kind of *malach* is Malachi referring?

Also, within the Book of Malachi, the prophet says the following about the ordained servants of God: "For the lips of a priest should guard knowledge, and people should seek instruction from his mouth, for he is the [*malach*] of the LORD of hosts" (2:7). One can see within the context of the verse itself what a *malach* is to do: to utter divine instruction with wise lips.

One might also mention a New Testament example. As with Hebrew, so with Greek: the word usually translated *angel* (*angelos*) merely means "messenger." Most New Testament instances of *angelos* do refer to those messengers who are heavenly beings. However, there is a long-standing interpretive tradition that understands the letters to the seven churches in Revelation, all of which are addressed to "the [*angelos*] of the church in ______," to be addressed to the *pastors* of the churches (2:1, 8, 12, 18; 3:1, 7, 14). Thus understood, these short letters are written to those who are called and ordained to be the messengers of the words of God, as were the priests of the Old Testament.

We see, therefore, that in the Old Testament, a *malach* is not necessarily an *angel*, with all the connotations that English word has attached to it. The *malach* of Yahweh is the mouthpiece of the Father. The importance of this cannot be overstated, for, as we will see, this *malach* who appeared to Moses in the burning bush is anything but a created heavenly being. How do we know that? Let's look at the rest of the verses to find our answer.

If *malach* simply means "messenger" or "spokesman," who is the *malach* in the bush? Read Exodus 3:1–6 again, very carefully. Note all the divine names that are used. Are any of these names applied to the *malach*? How does the *malach* describe himself in verse 6? What does that tell you about His identity?

Mark well what other divine names are mentioned in this encounter. When Moses says to himself that he is going to check out the bush, we read, "When the LORD [Yahweh] saw that he turned aside to see, God [*Elohim* in Hebrew] called to him out of the bush" (3:4). Two other divine names or titles are now connected with this *malach* in the bush: Yahweh and Elohim. (The Hebrew word *Elohim* is like the generic English word *God*; it is not really a name but a title or designation for the true deity, or, in some cases, false deities.) This verse does *not* say, "When the *malach* saw" but "when *Yahweh* saw that he turned aside." And, when Yahweh saw, "*Elohim* called to him out of the bush." So, who is in the bush: the *malach* of Yahweh, Yahweh Himself, or Elohim? We'll get to the answer in just a moment. After the One-in-the-bush tells Moses to take off his footgear, He identifies Himself: "I am the God [*Elohim*] of your father, the God [*Elohim*] of Abraham, the God [*Elohim*] of Isaac, and the God [*Elohim*] of Jacob" (3:6). Then, as if there were now any doubt, we see the telling response of Moses: "[He] hid his face, for he was afraid to look at God [*Elohim*]" (3:6).

Briefly look at other episodes where the *malach* of Yahweh appeared: Genesis 16:7–14; Genesis 22:11–18; Joshua 5:14; Judges 13:1–25. What do each of these tell you about the *malach's* identity? What does He do? By what names is He called?

So, now, let us answer the question: Who exactly is this *malach* in the bush anyway? He is the messenger of the Father; that much is unmistakable. But he is not only called *malach*; he is also referred to indirectly as Yahweh, and quite directly as *Elohim*. Who else is the messenger of the Father but also divine with the Father; One who speaks the words of God but is also God Himself; One by whom the Father reveals Himself throughout the Old Testament until finally He reveals Himself fully—who else could it be but the Christ, the divine Son? He is the *malach* of Yahweh. Such has been the confession of the church since the earliest days.

The church has, from her earliest days, identified the *malach* of Yahweh as the Son of God, who came down from heaven in Old Testament times disguised as an angel. Though He was not an angel, but divine and eternal, He would temporarily assume this form. How is this consistent with the Lord's presence in the church today? How is it different now and how is it the same?

Therefore, before "the Word became flesh and dwelt among us" (John 1:14), the Word already dwelt among us, that is, the Son dwelt among the people of His Father. Though not yet a flesh and blood man in the Old Testament, the Son of God would nevertheless frequently assume some kind of visible form, often that of a man or angel, to reveal Himself to people. For instance, in addition to appearing to Moses, He walked in the Garden of Eden to search for Adam and Eve (Genesis 3:8), and He appeared to Hagar as the "*malach* of God" (Genesis 16:7–14), to Abraham as the "*malach* of Yahweh" (Genesis 22:11–18), to Joshua as the "commander of the army of Yahweh" (Joshua 5:14), and as the "man of Yahweh" to Samson's parents (Judges 13:6, 8) and Ezekiel (Ezekiel 1:26–28). On each of these occasions, the divine Son temporarily appeared in some tangible, visible way to convey to an individual or group of individuals the message of His Father.

Within this fiery bush, therefore, Moses sees the One who will later be named Jesus. He came down from heaven to communicate with Moses from within this little tree. Not a creature, not a real angel, but God appeared. Disguised as an angel, camouflaged with fire, He opened His mouth to speak.

The Divine Fire

As you read through this story, you might be saying to yourself, "Okay, so God appears in the form of an angel. I can understand that. After all, He appears in all sorts of other ways also, like in clouds and on chariots and such. But why does He make this grand appearance from within this, well, ordinary piece of shrubbery? Isn't that sort of a weird location for God? And, what's more, why in the world is this shrub not only on fire, but on fire with flames that leave the bush unburned?" These questions lead us into some of the most fascinating parts of the story.

What are some other Old Testament accounts where the appearance of God, or specifically of His *malach,* are connected with fire? See Exodus 14:19–20; 19:18; Leviticus 9:24; Judges 13:20; Psalm 18:12–13; 50:3; 89:46.

Let's begin with the manner by which the divine presence is made known: in fire. The Son of God appeared to Moses "in a flame of fire out of the midst of the bush." For God to appear in some connection with fire is not that unusual in biblical stories. Possibly the first such account to come to mind is that of Pentecost. Then, on the heads of each of the apostles rested "divided tongues as of fire" (Acts 2:3). These fiery tongues were the outward manifestation of the Holy Spirit.

But there are plenty of other examples where God's appearance is linked with fire. Consider the following: When Israel marched out of Egypt into the wilderness, "the LORD went before them by day in a pillar of cloud to lead them along the way, and by night in a *pillar of fire* to give them light, that they might travel by day and by night" (Exodus 13:21, emphasis added). These, incidentally, are not two pillars but one; by day the pillar is a cloud and by night it is fire. It is also noteworthy that the *malach* of Yahweh (i.e., the Son of God), who appeared to Moses in the fiery bush, is also intimately connected with this fiery pillar (Exodus 14:19–20). When the Israelites arrived at Mount Sinai to receive the Ten Commandments and the other stipulations of the covenant, God again manifested Himself in fire: the mountain "was wrapped in smoke because the LORD had descended on it in fire" (Exodus 19:18). Later, when Aaron and his sons were ordained into the priesthood, "fire came out from before the LORD and consumed the burnt offering and the pieces of fat on the altar" (Leviticus 9:24). During the period of the judges, when the Son of God again appeared as the *malach* of Yahweh, this time to the parents of Samson, they offered a sacrifice to the LORD: "When the flame [of the sacrifice] went up toward heaven from the altar, the [*malach* of Yahweh] went up in the flame of the altar" (Judges 13:20). What a sight that must have been! The hymnal of Israel, the book of Psalms, is also full of verses that connect the Lord with fire: "coals of fire" accompany His appearance (18:12–13), before Him is a "devouring fire" (50:3), and His wrath "burns like fire" (89:46).

Where is fire connected with God's appearance in the New Testament? See Matthew 3:11; Acts 2:3; 2 Thessalonians 1:7–8; Revelation 1:14–15.

In addition to Pentecost, there are other places in the New Testament where fire and the divine presence are related. John the Baptist says Jesus will baptize "with the Holy Spirit and with fire" (Matthew 3:11). When our Lord returns on the Last Day, He will be "revealed from heaven with His mighty angels in flaming fire" (2 Thessalonians 1:7–8). The author of Hebrews, echoing Deuteronomy 4:24, describes God as a "consuming fire" (12:29). And finally, when the glorified Son of God appears to St. John at the beginning of Revelation, His "eyes were like a flame of fire" and "His feet were like burnished bronze, refined in a furnace" (1:14–15).

What is the message conveyed by this close connection of God with fire? What purposes—negative or positive—does fire serve in ordinary circumstances? Do these ordinary purposes help us to understand why God appears in fire? Why or why not?

Clearly, God and fire are not loosely related in the biblical account. Far from it! Fire or flames are one of the most widespread ways in which the divine presence is made visible to His people. But why is this? How does fire serve as such an apt visualization for God's revelation?

What do the following passages tell us about the negative purpose of the God-and-fire connection? Deuteronomy 4:24; Hebrews 12:29; Psalm 97:3.

The reason is twofold, both negative and positive, and has to do with the nature of fire. First, as fire enflames and eventually destroys materials that are contrary to itself, so, as we saw above, "our God is a consuming fire" (Deuteronomy 4:24; Hebrews 12:29). "Fire goes before Him and burns up His adversaries all around" (Psalm 97:3), and His wrath "burns like fire" (Psalm 89:46). Thus hell—that ultimate and everlasting place of divine wrath—is called the "lake of fire" into which unbelievers are thrown for their rejection of Christ (Revelation 20:14–15).

What do the following passages tell us about the positive purpose of the connection? Exodus 13:21; Daniel 11:33–35; Malachi 3:2–3; Acts 2:3.

Besides this negative reason, however, there is also a positive one. For fire not only destroys, but it also provides light, purification, and protection, like our loving God does for His people. He clothed Himself in the pillar of fire to give light to the Israelites (Exodus 13:21), as well as to protect them from the Egyptians when they pursued them to the shore of the Red Sea (14:19–20). Later, He sent His Spirit in tongues of fire to the apostles so that they might know foreign tongues of speech (i.e., languages) by which they might preach the Good News of salvation in the crucified and resurrected Messiah. Moreover, just as fire purifies metals such as silver and gold by burning away the worthless dross clinging to them, thereby improving these metals, so our Lord refines His children, burning away by various disciplines the dross of sin that clings to us (Daniel 11:33–35; Zechariah 13:9; Malachi 3:2–3; cf. Hebrews 12:3–11). Although such refinements are a "fiery trial," as Peter calls them (1 Peter 4:12), they are prompted by the goodness and concern of our heavenly Father, who "disciplines the one He loves" (Hebrews 12:6).

Now, let us reflect again upon the fire in the burning bush. This fire is the fire of the *malach* of Yahweh, the "angelic clothing," if you will, by which the Son of God manifests Himself to Moses. Later, the Son will again wrap Himself in fire—in the pillar of fire which leads the nation out of Egypt. Fire is thus the element of creation chosen by Christ to make His invisible nature visible. As we saw in Revelation, even after His incarnation, the Son of God continues to reveal Himself in connection with fire, since He has eyes like a flame of fire and feet like bronze that has been burned in fire (1:14–15). At His transfiguration, Jesus must also have exhibited a bodily appearance that was fiery, for His face "shone like the sun" (Matthew 17:2) and "His clothes became radiant" (Mark 9:3).

Is the appearance of the Son of God in fire within the burning bush a positive or negative message? Had He come to announce punishment and wrath or something else?

Is this fiery revelation of God at the burning bush positive or negative? The answer to that question is clear from the words to Moses. For the Son of God did not come down to chastise Moses or announce His wrath against Israel. Rather, He appeared to say that He had seen the affliction of His people, heard their cry, and was acting to deliver them (Exodus 3:7–8). This was a revelation of grace and salvation. In the deep, dark night of their suffering, the light of God would shine. He was coming to save His own, to be wrathful fire against Egypt but loving fire for Israel.

The Created Bush

Be honest: If you had to pick a spot in creation for God to manifest Himself, where would it be? That God should choose a simple bush tells us something about Him and His ways—what is it?

Read Isaiah 45:15. How does the prophet describe the Lord? He is the God who does what? Give examples of how this is seen, either in the Bible or in the church today.

When the chosen nation arrived at Sinai after three months of journeying from Egypt, they saw quite a sight: "There were thunders and lightnings and a thick cloud on the mountain and a very loud trumpet blast, so that all the people in the camp trembled. . . . Now Mount Sinai was wrapped in smoke because the LORD had descended on it in fire. The smoke of it went up like the smoke of a kiln, and the whole mountain trembled greatly" (Exodus 19:16,18). Not a soul was unmoved by this tremendous display of divine power—people and earth are quaking in fright! That was Sinai when the whole nation was there, but what about Sinai when only Moses was there? In Exodus 19 it must have looked like the end of the world was at hand, but in Exodus 3 there's only this little bush aflame. Now, of course, this in itself was quite fascinating, certainly curious enough to draw Moses away from his sheep to get a closer look. But it did not have all those awe-inspiring, fear-provoking phenomena that the later divine appearance at Sinai had. There was, well, a bush, a piece of shrubbery, on fire. Only this, nothing more. Doesn't this seem sort of—what shall we say?—beneath God, too simple and down-to-earth for the God of gods and Lord of lords?

The simple answer is "yes," it certainly does seem to be a rather unworthy throne for the almighty God. Without a doubt, were we to pick a place for God to reveal Himself, we would at least pick a huge boulder, immense oak, or something like that—a piece of creation with more style than a dwarfed tree. But there we go again, thinking like fallen creatures instead of like the One in whom all wisdom resides. His thoughts are not our thoughts, His ways not our ways (Isaiah 55:8–9). He is, as the prophet Isaiah says, the *God who hides Himself* (45:15). God hides Himself in things that, to us sinners, seem "un-godlike," not fit for His majesty, too poor for His richness, too weak for His strength. But that is His way. He does it quite on purpose, for "God chose what is foolish in the world to shame the wise; God chose what is weak in the world to shame the strong; God chose what is low and despised in the world, even things that are not, to bring to nothing things that are, so that no human being might boast in the presence of God" (1 Corinthians 1:27–29). Our Lord camouflages Himself, to be sure, but He does so only to hide Himself from those who want a god that bedazzles the world with all kinds of fanfare. Though disguised in simplicity, He is still readily perceptible to those who know where to find Him, who believe that He truly is where He has promised to be: in His Word, His Baptism, His Holy Communion.

So there He is before Moses, in the bush. In that plain, ordinary, down-to-earth shrub is God in all His fullness. Who would have guessed it? No one, and that's the point. Our Lord conforms only to His own standards. Yes, of course, there are times, such as later at Sinai, when God really wows everyone by such an awesome appearance. But these appearances are not the rule; they are the exception, the very rare exception indeed.

The rule is simplicity. The rule is plainness. The rule is God-in-the-bush. And that rule of lowliness holds true as much in the New Testament as it does in the Old. The reality is that when God begins something, it almost always seems as if nothing will come of it. Just consider the life of our Lord. He's conceived inside the womb of some unknown peasant girl in the boondocks of Israel. One of the first smells to fill His nostrils is the dung of cattle and sheep. Before He's even walking, a king tries to murder Him, thus forcing Him and His family to become refugees in Egypt. The world is virtually ignorant of His existence for the first 30 years of His life; He's just one of the millions of Jews being lorded over by the Romans. Even when He begins His ministry, things don't improve. Mourners stop their wailing to laugh at Him, His townsfolk try to throw Him off a cliff, His family thinks He's gone mad, and the big chiefs in Jerusalem want Him dead, the sooner the better. At the end, when He's arrested, tried in a monkey court, and sentenced to hang from the nails, His followers become turncoats, crowds mock, and, except for a few women gathered around the cross, He's abandoned by everyone. Even His corpse has to be laid in a borrowed tomb. This, dear reader, is lowliness, simplicity, the "foolishness" of our Lord (as St. Paul calls it).

Yet the appearance was not the reality. For defeat was really victory, death was life, and crucifixion became resurrection. He who was, by all accounts, only a man, was revealed to be a man who is simultaneously God in the flesh. His rejection was our acceptance by the Father. His death is our life. He gave up everything, that He might bestow it all upon us. This He did, all while He was hiding Himself. He was the Father's only-begotten Son, loved by the Father, worshiped by angels, the Creator of heaven and earth, yet He wore our skin. Even though flesh and blood was His camouflage, however, it was not the kind a soldier or hunter puts on, then later takes off. He *became* flesh and blood permanently, everlastingly. His camouflage is now His human nature, inseparably bound to His divine nature. He is one person, who is both divine with the Father and human with us.

Throughout the history of the church, preachers have used the burning bush as an illustration of the incarnation. What are the parallels between these two events? What do both tell us, for example, about the earthly and the heavenly coming together, about what the divine does to the created? Where does the illustration break down?

This God-man is the same one who, absent His humanity, appeared to Moses in the burning bush. Not in flesh and blood yet, but only in fire, He dwelt in that shrub. And the bush was not eaten up by the flames. It remained intact, burning with fire but not burned to ashes. Such an image—that of a created thing filled with, but not consumed by, the uncreated God—has been a favorite illustration throughout the history of the church for our Lord's incarnation. Why is that? How is the burning bush an image of God becoming man?

When the Son of God "came down from heaven and was incarnate by the Holy Spirit of the Virgin Mary" (Nicene Creed), He became all man, fully human, with a body and soul like we have. That which was of the earth (human nature) was filled with that which is of heaven (divine nature). The two natures, God's and man's, were joined together in this one unique person, the Son of God.

In an analogous way, the fire of divinity was enclosed within the natural bush on Mount Sinai. That which was of the earth (the bush) was filled with that which is of heaven (the fiery Son of God). Moreover, the fire of divinity did not destroy the bush. Though fire, of course, usually burns up every tree or shrub with which it comes into contact, this bush "was burning, yet it was not consumed" (3:2). It was unharmed. Similarly, when the Son of God took upon Himself our human nature from the womb of the Virgin Mary, He did not destroy that human nature. The fire of His divinity did not destroy or harm in any way our flesh. Rather, the flesh benefited from such a union! Because His flesh and blood are not only human, but actually God's own flesh and God's own blood, they participate in what is divine. For this reason, Jesus says, "Truly, truly, I say to you, unless you eat the flesh of the Son of Man and drink His blood, you have no life in you. Whoever feeds on My flesh and drinks My blood has eternal life, and I will raise him up on the last day. For My flesh is true food, and My blood is true drink. Whoever feeds on My flesh and drinks My blood abides in Me, and I in him" (John 6:53–56). Without a doubt, no other man could claim that about His flesh and blood, but Jesus can. For His flesh is God's flesh and His blood divine blood. Since God is life, God's flesh and blood bestow life upon those who eat and drink them.

What Moses the shepherd saw on Mount Sinai is therefore like what other shepherds beheld in Bethlehem 14 hundred years later. Moses saw the Son of God, united temporarily with a natural bush;

the shepherds saw the Son of God, united permanently with a natural body. Though His infant flesh was not glowing with the fiery light of divinity like it later would atop the Mount of Transfiguration, that divine fire was already there. In the burning bush, therefore, we see a preview of the incarnation of the *malach* of Yahweh, the Son and Messenger of the Father.

Conclusion

In the Garden of Eden, we first encounter the God who likes to work through trees. In Exodus, on the peak of Sinai, we see that God still likes to work through trees. Though the burning bush was probably not nearly as outwardly lovely as the Tree of Life and the Tree of the Knowledge of Good and Evil, it nonetheless communicated a most beautiful message. That message is that the God of love who formed Adam and Eve, who called Abraham, and who made great promises to Isaac and Jacob, had not forgotten His people. He came down from heaven and became present in the burning bush to tell Moses of His concern. He sent that shepherd back to Egypt to lead His people out of slavery and to the Promised Land. This revelation of God once again shows that God is not a hands-off deity who wants nothing to do with His creation. Quite the opposite: He comes down from above, He makes Himself visible, He speaks, and He listens. He acts out of love and compassion. He does all this from a simple bush. As later, when He permanently united our created nature with His divinity, so here He places His divine presence in something of the earth. That is the way of our God, who always chooses that which seems unworthy of Him, to give us, His people, that which we so desperately need. Thanks be to Him!

Closing Prayer

"O Adonai and ruler of the house of Israel, who appeared to Moses in the burning bush and gave him the Law on Sinai: Come with an outstretched arm and redeem us." Amen.

(Antiphon for December 18, *LW*, p. 288)

THE BURNING BUSH

The God of Revelation

Do most people think that God is near or far from His creation? How do they think He interacts with it, if He does at all? With what do they associate His appearances? How might their view of how God reveals Himself affect their view of Him?

Think of incidents in the Bible when God revealed Himself to people. How did He appear, for example, to Adam and Eve in the garden **(Genesis 3:8)**; to Abraham **(Genesis 15:12–21)**; to the Israelites at Mount Sinai **(Exodus 19–20)**; to Jesus at His Baptism **(Matthew 3:13–17)**? What is similar and what is different about these incidents?

Read **Colossians 2:9**. What does Paul say about where we see the full revelation of God? Why is this so important?

The Shepherd Moses

Review the history of Israel from the last few chapters of Genesis to the second chapter of Exodus. How did Jacob and his children end up in Egypt? What happened to them when there—both good and bad? What caused Pharaoh to begin his murderous cleansing? How was Moses rescued? Where did he grow up? How did he end up a refugee?

The Mountain of God

Read **Exodus 3 (especially vv. 1–6)**. In what vocation was Moses engaged when the Lord appeared to him? What did the Lord call him to do? Compare **Exodus 3:1** with Psalm **77:20**. How was Moses called from one vocation to a similar vocation? How did the Lord Jesus work in a similar way with Matthew **(Matthew 9:9–13)** as well as with Peter, Andrew, James, and John **(Matthew 4:18–22)**? Matthew was called from handling money to handling what kind of treasure? Peter and the other men were called to become what kind of fishermen?

Why is Horeb, or Sinai, called the "mountain of God"? What made it especially *God's* mountain? Compare this terminology with similar phrases elsewhere in the Bible. For instance, fill in "the ______ of God" with the aid of the following verses: **Ezekiel 28:13**; **Psalm 46:4**; 1 **Chronicles 6:48**. What makes each of these special?

Is sacred space still important in the church? Why or why not?

For Old Testament believers, the temple was the place where they went to be in God's presence, to hear His Word, to receive His gifts. Where does Jesus say our temple is now (**John 2:21**)? How do we enter this new "temple"?

Read **Hebrews 12:22–24**. What and where is this "Mount Zion"? Note the tense of the verbs: are they past tense or future tense? That is, have we *already come* or *will* we come? How does this section help us to answer the question of the importance of sacred space in the church?

The *Malach* of Yahweh

Read **Exodus 3:2**. Who appears to Moses in the burning bush? What do you think of when the word *angel* is spoken? The Hebrew word used here is *malach*. Though it is usually translated as angel, the word simply means "messenger."

Now turn to the last book of the Old Testament—Malachi. The name of this prophet simply means "My *malach,*" that is, "My messenger." Read **Malachi 2:7**. Most English translations will render the last part of the verse as "he is the messenger of the LORD of hosts." The Hebrew word is again *malach*. To what kind of *malach* is Malachi referring?

If *malach* simply means "messenger" or "spokesman," who is the *malach* in the bush? Read **Exodus 3:1–6** again, very carefully. Note all the divine names that are used. Are any of these names applied to the *malach*? How does the *malach* describe himself in verse 6? What does that tell you about His identity?

Briefly look at other episodes where the *malach* of Yahweh appeared: **Genesis 16:7–14; Genesis 22:11–18; Joshua 5:14; Judges 13:1–25**. What do each of these tell you about the *malach's* identity? What does He do? By what names is He called?

The church has, from her earliest days, identified the *malach* of Yahweh as the Son of God, who came down from heaven in Old Testament times disguised as an angel. Though He was not an angel, but divine and eternal, He would temporarily assume this form. How is this consistent with the Lord's presence in the church today? How is it different now and how is it the same?

The Divine Fire

What are some other Old Testament accounts where the appearance of God, or specifically of His *malach,* are connected with fire? See **Exodus 14:19–20; 19:18; Leviticus 9:24; Judges 13:20; Psalm 18:12–13; 50:3; 89:46.**

Where is fire connected with God's appearance in the New Testament? See **Matthew 3:11; Acts 2:3; 2 Thessalonians 1:7–8; Revelation 1:14–15**.

What is the message conveyed by this close connection of God with fire? What purposes—negative or positive—does fire serve in ordinary circumstances? Do these ordinary purposes help us to understand why God appears in fire? Why or why not?

What do the following passages tell us about the negative purpose of the God-and-fire connection? **Deuteronomy 4:24; Hebrews 12:29; Psalm 97:3**.

What do the following passages tell us about the positive purpose of the connection? **Exodus 13:21; Daniel 11:33–35; Malachi 3:2–3; Acts 2:3**.

Is the appearance of the Son of God in fire within the burning bush a positive or negative message? Had He come to announce punishment and wrath or something else?

The Created Bush

Be honest: If you had to pick a spot in creation for God to manifest Himself, where would it be? That God should choose a simple bush tells us something about Him and His ways—what is it?

Read **Isaiah 45:15**. How does the prophet describe the Lord? He is the God who does what? Give examples of how this is seen, either in the Bible or in the church today.

Throughout the history of the church, preachers have used the burning bush as an illustration of the incarnation. What are the parallels between these two events? What do both tell us, for example, about the earthly and the heavenly coming together, about what the divine does to the created? Where does the illustration break down?

3

The Staff of Moses

Prayer

Almighty God, our Maker and Redeemer, who sent Your servant Moses down into Egypt to deliver Israel from the hand of Pharaoh with a staff of wood, and who sent Your Son, Jesus Christ, down from heaven to deliver all mankind from bondage to the devil upon the wood of the cross, look with pity upon us and rescue us from all our adversaries; through the same, Jesus Christ, Your Son, our Lord. Amen.

The Underdog

What are some biblical stories that come to mind in which the main character is an underdog? See, for example, Judges 6–7 and 1 Samuel 17. What kinds of odds do these people face? What are their enemies like?

If there were ever a collection of historical tales in which the underdog is a principal character in story after story, that collection would have to be the Bible. Although there are exceptions here and there, more often than not, the reader of the Scriptures encounters battles in which the proverbial "99-pound weakling" is pitted against the weight-lifting jock with arms the size of tree trunks. The odds are stacked against him. He's dead meat. He doesn't stand a snowball's chance in you-know-where. Page after page of the Bible is filled with stories such as these.

Right at the top of the list, of course, is the battle of David and Goliath. There goes the teenager from Bethlehem, still wet behind the ears, armed with that not-so-scary weapon called the slingshot. He's got five rocks in his pouch, but he'd be much better off with five machine guns strapped on his back, considering the giant who's walking toward him. But David marches onward, undaunted by either the mocking laughter of Goliath or his own battlefield inexperience. The young shepherd has Yahweh on his side; that's all he needs to steel him with courage. And, sure enough, the fight is over before it has even begun, as a single rock sails through the air from David's sling to bury itself in Goliath's big head. Down, down he tumbles, the monster slain by the youth. The underdog claims the victory.

In addition to David, there's the underdog Gideon, who goes to battle against thousands upon thousands of Midianites, Amalekites, and the sons of the east (Judges 6–8). In this case, God makes sure Gideon will be the underdog. First, He reduces Gideon's multi-thousand man fighting force to a mere three hundred. Then, He tells him to leave all the regular weapons at home. No need for bows, arrows, swords, or spears. Not even slingshots are necessary in this fight. All they need are trumpets, torches, and clay jars. Under cover of darkness, Gideon and his band surround the camp of the enemy, smash the jars, hold up the torches, and fill the night air with the sound of horns. Up springs the sleeping enemy. Bewildered and frightened, they turn not on the Israelites, but upon each other. Midianites kill Midianites, Amalekites kill Amalekites. It's a bloody mess. Gideon and his men stand back and virtually trumpet forth taps for the self-made funeral of their enemies. Without even unsheathing a sword, the underdogs win once again.

The stories go on and on. The weak defeat the strong; the worldly foolish overcome the worldly wise; youth and inexperience triumph over age and skill. The underdog has his day, while those we expect to win skulk away wounded and bleeding, or bite the dust of death.

What kinds of weapons are used by these underdogs? How would you characterize these weapons? See also the accounts in Judges 3:31; 15:15.

Why would God place weapons such as these in the hands of these underdogs? See Psalm 44:6–7.

One of the most intriguing aspects of such underdog stories are the weapons used in the fights. David has his sling. Gideon has his trumpets, jars, and torches. The judge Shamgar single-handedly struck down six hundred Philistines with an oxgoad (Judges 3:31), while Samson outdid him with the jawbone of a donkey (Judges 15:15). The point of such silly weaponry is expressed very well by the psalmist, who prays: "For not in my bow do I trust, nor can my sword save me. But You have saved us from our foes and have put to shame those who hate us" (Psalm 44:6–7). The weapons of the underdogs are not really even their slings, trumpets, or oxgoads. In truth, their weapon is none other than God Himself. He uses the seemingly foolish armaments—but the power of such weak arms is the strong Word of God attached to them. The divine Word of promised victory wrapped around the slingshot and the donkey jawbone endow such weapons with the might of Yahweh. Each of them becomes, in the hand of the underdog, the sling of God, the trumpet of God, the oxgoad of the Almighty.

So it was also in the case of another bizarre weapon: the staff of Moses. As we will see, this piece of wood in the hand of this 80-year-old man was more than a simple shepherd's crook. It became—like David's sling—the weapon that brought that Goliath of a nation called Egypt crashing to the ground.

What Is That in Your Hand?

Read Exodus 3–4. As God begins to outline His mission to Moses, how does Moses react? See Exodus 3:11, 13; 4:1, 10, 13.

In the last lesson, we discussed the burning bush, in which the angel of the Lord (in truth, the Son of God *disguised* as an angel) appeared to Moses. As the messenger of the Father begins to outline the mission on which He is sending Moses, this shepherd begins to protest. Question after question begins to fill his mind. He starts with his own lowliness, "Who am I that I should go to Pharaoh and bring the children of Israel out of Egypt?" (Exodus 3:11). The Lord basically tells him, "No need to worry. I will go with you. I'll do the work." Next Moses asks, "If I come to the people of Israel and say to them, 'The God of your fathers has sent me to you,' and they ask me, 'What is His name?' what shall I say to them?" (Exodus 3:13). God has an answer for that as well: "I AM WHO I AM" (Exodus 3:14). Significantly, from these words in Hebrew we get the divine name *Yahweh*, which essentially means, "He is who He is."

How does God respond to Moses' question in Exodus 4:1? What message is sent by this miracle?

But Moses is not yet finished. He has more questions—each of which, by the way, begins to resemble more of a protest than a real question. He goes on: "But behold, they will not believe me or listen to my voice, for they will say, 'The LORD did not appear to you' " (Exodus 4:1). Moses is worried about his credibility. What if he goes all the way to Egypt and risks his own neck—remember he is, according to Egyptian law, still an outlaw—and his own people laugh him out of town? What if they don't believe that Yahweh really appeared to him and sent him on this mission? How will he be able to prove his legitimacy?

The answer to the question of Moses begins with a question from God:

> *"What is that in your hand?" He said, "A staff." And He said, "Throw it on the ground." So he threw it on the ground, and it became a serpent, and Moses ran from it. But the LORD said to Moses, "Put out your hand and catch it by the tail"—so he put out his hand and caught it, and it became a staff in his hand—"that they may believe that the LORD, the God of their fathers, the God of Abraham, the God of Isaac, and the God of Jacob, has appeared to you." (Exodus 4:2–5)*

What is this, you might be asking yourself, a class called Snake-Handling 101? By no means. Rather, this is to be a sign that Moses has truly been called by God to bring about freedom for the people of Israel. It is a sign "that they may believe." First of all, we must note the obvious fact that what has just taken place is a miracle. It is not magic. Later, as we will see, Pharaoh's men will *magically* transform their staffs into snakes (Exodus 7:8–13). But the staff of Moses is transformed not by sleight of hand or devilish trickery. It becomes something new solely by the Word of God. This is the beginning of many instances in which God will endow this simple piece of wood with supernatural powers—powers that are brought about because of divine speech.

With what event is the serpent most closely associated in the Bible (Genesis 3)? Since this

snake is transformed back into a staff by the hand of Moses, might this reversal (from something bad to something good) indicate something else that the Lord will soon reverse? How is the slavery in Egypt related to the work of the devil?

When we hear about a serpent in the Scriptures, we cannot but think about the serpent in the Garden of Eden. From Genesis to Revelation, the snake is associated with the fall of mankind into sin. So we may think of it here as well. Israel's enslavement in Egypt is one example of how much Satan and sin corrupted the world. God did not make His people to be slaves, but to be free, freely serving Him and their neighbors. Thus God, in love, desired to rescue them, to reverse what Satan (through Pharaoh) had done. This He would accomplish through the man Moses, specifically, through the staff of Moses. By this piece of wood God would bring plagues upon Egypt, divide the Red Sea, bring back the waters upon the Egyptians, and bring water out of the rock in the desert.

In this miracle of a serpent turning back into a staff when Moses grabs it with his hand, we have a preview of how God is going to work. He will turn back the work of the serpent of hell, restoring Israel to what they were meant to be, even as He turns the serpentine staff back into a wooden shepherd's crook once again. This common piece of wood in the hand of Israel's redeemer would restore the people of God.

Read Exodus 4:18–20. Is this the same staff? Now to whom does the staff belong? What does this tell you about the purpose of the staff? Discuss other examples in Scripture in which the Lord claims something common, ordinary, and down-to-earth as His own? How is the "staff of God" related to these? What does this tell us about how God desires to work in this world?

When Moses has finally exhausted every possible excuse he could come up with—and exhausted the patience of the Lord in the process (Exodus 4:14)!—he prepared to head down to Egypt. The final words God speaks to him from the burning bush are these: "Take in your hand this staff, with which you shall do the signs" (Exodus 4:17). That Moses does so, we are told shortly thereafter, although with a slight *but very important change* in language: "So Moses took his wife and his sons and had them ride on a donkey, and went back to the land of Egypt. And Moses took the *staff of God* in his hand" (Exodus 4:20, emphasis added). The "staff of God"? Wait a minute! Did God just hand over a new staff, plopped down from the celestial heights, crafted from heavenly timber? No, Moses is still holding his own, common staff. It is his inasmuch as he owned it, used it as a shepherd's crook, carried it with him to Mount Sinai, and so forth. But now it is also, and most important, the staff of God. It is God's, however, not so much because He created that piece of wood—although, of course, He did—but because when He called Moses, He claimed that staff as His own. He made it holy, that is, made it His unique instrument, set it apart, specially designated it for a divine purpose. Henceforth, it will belong not only to Moses, but to God. God will use it as the tool of rescue for His people. It will become, as it were, the visible symbol of the arm of the Lord, by which He mightily redeems Israel.

The Snake Staff

Read Exodus 5. What kind of reception do Moses and Aaron receive from Pharaoh? How does Pharaoh respond to their request? How does Pharaoh set the other Israelites against Moses and Aaron?

When Moses arrived in Egypt, things did not go very well at first. In fact, they went really, really badly. Moses and his brother Aaron appeared before the king of Egypt to relay the demand of Yahweh—that Pharaoh let the Israelites go out to the wilderness to celebrate a feast to Him (Exodus 5:1–5). Pharaoh did everything but laugh at their request. He scoffed that he did not even know who Yahweh was. The request was—in his eyes—ludicrous. There was no way he was going to let his slaves have a religious holiday.

Then, to add insult to injury, Pharaoh slyly set

the Israelites against Moses and Aaron. He took away the straw he had been providing for the production of bricks, while stipulating that the people must still make just as many bricks as before. So the Israelites scattered here and there, frantically searching for straw, while still trying to keep up with the quota of bricks. When some of the leaders were beaten because the people made fewer bricks than required, they complained to Pharaoh, who used the occasion to point an accusing finger at Moses and Aaron. The leaders, angry and hurt, verbally assaulted Moses and his brother, telling them, "The LORD look on you and judge, because you have made us stink in the sight of Pharaoh and his servants, and have put a sword in their hand to kill us" (Exodus 5:21). Needless to say, it was not a good start. Soon thereafter, however, it began to be obvious that Pharaoh would be forced to listen to Moses and Yahweh, whether he was willing to do so or not.

Read Exodus 7:1–13. What does Aaron do with the staff? Why does he do it, that is, what message does this send to the Egyptians? What do the Egyptians do with their staffs? Are these two transformations exactly the same? How was the source behind the change in the rod of Aaron different from the source behind the change in the rods of the Egyptians? Why is this distinction all-important?

Some time later, Moses and Aaron went back to Pharaoh, this time loaded for bear. They:

> *Went to Pharaoh and did just as the Lord commanded. Aaron cast down his staff before Pharaoh and his servants, and it became a serpent. Then Pharaoh summoned the wise men and the sorcerers, and they, the magicians of Egypt, also did the same by their secret arts. For each man cast down his staff, and they became serpents. But Aaron's staff swallowed up their staffs. (Exodus 7:10–12)*

You might have thought this miraculous sign would break through the leader's stony heart, but, alas, it didn't even make a dent. "Still Pharaoh's heart was hardened, and he would not listen to them, as the LORD had said" (Exodus 7:13).

This miracle is similar to the divine sign God had given to Moses at Mount Sinai, with which he was to convince the Israelites that Yahweh had truly sent him. This miracle before Pharaoh and his servants, however, was designed to convince the enemies of God that Yahweh alone was the true God and that they should obey His Word. That the sorcerers of Egypt were able seemingly to imitate the sign given by Moses and Aaron is not too surprising. Whether by magical art, trickery, or actual satanic power they produced something like that which Moses did. But how they *did* it is not nearly as important as how they *did not* do it; they did not do it through the Word of God, as Moses and Aaron did. That distinction makes all the difference. Even though they could in some way replicate the miracle, as indeed they did again later with the first two plagues (Exodus 7:22; 8:7), these were, in the end, only human fabrications, bound ultimately to fail. They were not divine miracles brought about by the ever-sure Word of the Father, as were the miracles of Moses.

Compare the swallowing of the Egyptians' staffs with the later "swallowing" that took place at the Red Sea (Exodus 15:10–12). How was this incident in Pharaoh's palace a preview of what would later happen?

In what way did Pharaoh react to this event?

The superior nature of the miracle over the human trick was proven decisively when the staff of Aaron swallowed up the staffs of the Egyptian magicians. There is no reason, by the way, to doubt that the staff of Aaron is actually the same as the staff of Moses and of God. In some places, it is called the staff of Moses, in others the staff of Aaron or God, but it is all the same rod. Here and elsewhere, it is called Aaron's staff because he was acting as the "prophet of Moses," standing alongside him since Moses had refused to follow fully what God had earlier called him to do (Exodus 4:14–17). This "swallowing" by Aaron's staff was itself prophetic of what was later to happen at the Red Sea. When Israel crossed over, with their former enemies floating dead onto the seashore, they sang of how God had given them victory:

You blew with Your wind; the sea covered them; they sank like lead in the mighty waters. Who is like You, O LORD, among the gods? Who is like You, majestic in holiness, awesome in glorious deeds, doing wonders? You stretched out Your right hand; the earth swallowed them. *(Exodus 15:10–12, emphasis added)*

As when the serpentine rod of Aaron swallowed the Egyptian rods, the superiority of Israel's God—the only true God—was made clear. So the message was also clear at the Red Sea: there is no one like Yahweh among the gods of the Egyptians or any other heathen. If Pharaoh had listened to Moses or heeded the miracle, he and his men would not later have been swallowed in death.

The Plaguing Staff

When Pharaoh hardened his heart against the clear message and sign God had given through His servants, the Lord began to play hardball. As He had predicted, this leader would refuse and refuse and refuse—until finally he had no other option but to submit to the Word of God. In response to Pharaoh's steadfast unwillingness to listen, the Lord began to send multiple plagues upon Egypt. In many of these, if not all of them, the staff of Moses was the icon of God's hand or God's arm striking the land.

Read Exodus 7:14–25. How was the staff of Moses used in this first plague? How does Pharaoh react to this?

In the first plague, God instructed Moses to meet Pharaoh at the Nile River in the morning when he came out to bathe. He was to take in hand the staff that had turned into a serpent. First, he was to declare to Pharaoh that, even though God had expressly commanded that he let the Israelites go, he had refused to obey the divine Word. Then, he was to announce the impending punishment for such disregard of the Word of God.

By this you shall know that I am the LORD: behold, with the staff that is in my hand I will strike the water that is in the Nile, and it shall turn into blood. The fish in the Nile shall die, and the Nile will stink, and the Egyptians will grow weary of drinking water from the Nile. (Exodus 7:17–18)

So Moses—having forewarned Pharaoh—struck the Nile with the staff and, lo and behold, the water throughout Egypt reddened into blood. Even in the face of this plague, however, Pharaoh was unmoved. "[He] turned and went into his house, and he did not take even this to heart" (Exodus 7:23).

Read Exodus 8:1–15. How is this plague similar yet different from the first one? What purpose does the divine staff serve?

Seven days later (Exodus 7:25), along came plague number two. Once more, God gave the Egyptian leader a chance to have a change of heart, to relinquish his slavish hold upon the Lord's chosen nation, and let them go free. Although Pharaoh's refusal is not expressly cited, he must have treated this threat with the same contempt with which he treated the first plague, since the plague befell the land. This second divine attack involved frogs—lots and *lots* of frogs. Like the first, it was initiated with the staff of Moses and God. This time Aaron (not Moses) stretched out the divine rod over the rivers, canals, and pools of Egypt. Like honey draws flies, so the rod drew forth the frogs. The whole land was overrun with these slimy animals. No place was untouched. They hopped into houses and beds, ovens and kneading bowls. Now Pharaoh began to take at least a little notice of Moses and Aaron. Although not repentant, he did ask them to plead with God to remove the "omnipresent" amphibians. This they did. The frogs died and were gathered together in heaps. With millions of their rotting little corpses lying around in piles, the land stank to high heaven. But, once more, as soon as Pharaoh saw that he was temporarily off the hook, he hardened his heart and closed his ears to God's spokesmen.

Read Exodus 8:16–19. What does Aaron do with the staff this time? What pattern has developed relative to the warning and inflicting of the plague? In what way is the reaction of the magicians different with regard to this plague?

Then the third plague came. By now the pattern was set. God tells Moses to do such-and-such with his staff, he does it, and *wham!* The land is hit with another blow from above. In this case, God tells Moses to tell Aaron to strike the dust of Egypt with the now famous staff. This being done, the dust of the earth became gnats in all the land of Egypt (Exodus 8:16). With this plague, pressure began to mount against the Egyptian king, for even the magicians couldn't imitate this miracle with their secret arts. They told Pharaoh, "This is the finger of God," but Pharaoh virtually shook a fist full of fingers at heaven, still persisting in his rebellion.

In the fourth (flies), fifth (pestilence), and sixth (boils) plagues, no mention is made of the staff. But it is used again in the seventh (Exodus 9:23) and eighth plagues (Exodus 10:12–13). How would you characterize its use in each of these plagues? How else might God have brought down these plagues upon Egypt? That He did not merely speak His Word, but used a staff, informs us about how God works. What kinds of "staffs" might God use today to punish people or nations?

In the fourth, fifth, and sixth plagues (flies, pestilence, and boils), there is no explicit mention of the staff of Moses, though, given the precedent set already, it may have been used there as well. Reference is made to it again in the seventh plague, when the Lord rained down hail upon Egypt: "Moses stretched out his staff toward heaven, and the LORD sent thunder and hail, and fire ran down to the earth" (Exodus 9:23). Similarly, in the eighth plague, when Moses stretched out his staff over the land of Egypt, the Lord brought an east wind that carried with it devouring locusts (Exodus 10:12–13). In the ninth and final plague, the staff goes unmentioned.

It is noteworthy in each of these instances that, even though the miracles differ from one another, each of them is effected in the same way: by God's Word operating through the staff. The Lord does not merely boom His voice down from heaven to warn Pharaoh about what He is about to do. Nor does Moses merely use his lips to call forth the frogs, gnats, hail, or some other catastrophic plague from water or out of the blue. Instead, he raises his staff skyward, or strikes water or earth with it to begin the affliction. The miracle, though negative, is generated by this common piece of wood, endowed with power from on high.

When Jesus performed miracles in the New Testament, they were not plagues. They were typically healings or other kinds of blessings. What does this tell us about the purpose of our Lord's coming (see John 3:16–17)?

We see something of a parallel to this in various miracles of the New Testament as well. There is first of all a contrast to observe. The vast majority of New Testament miracles are positive in nature, that is, they effect good for a person or group of people. Jesus never calls down a plague upon His enemies. Indeed, when some of His disciples are irked at a village of Samaritans for not receiving Jesus, they want to call fire down from heaven to consume the rebels. Rather than yielding to such a desire, Jesus instead rebukes His disciples and continues His journey to Jerusalem. The truth is that *Jesus Himself* will be the object of the divine wrath that was behind all the plagues that hit Egypt. On the cross, He will endure what all of us "Egyptians" deserve; there He is "plagued" with our punishments!

Moses had his staff—a created object—for these miracles of punishment. What kinds of created materials did Jesus use for his miracles of grace? See John 9:6; Mark 8:5, 23; Matthew 14:13–21.

What kinds of miracles take place every Lord's Day in the Divine Service? What created objects does Jesus use to perform these miracles?

There is, however, a similarity between these 10 miraculous plagues upon Pharaoh and the numerous miracles performed by our Lord Jesus: in both Testaments God works His miracles via certain things. In the Egyptian plagues, He used the staff of Moses. In His ministry Jesus healed a blind man with mud made from His own saliva (John 9:6); He also spit on another man's eyes to heal them (Mark 8:23). He provided food for 5,000+ people once and 4,000+ another time by multiplying food that was already present (Matthew 14:13–21; 15:32–39). In many miracles, He used His own hands as the divine instrument attached to His Word (e.g., Matthew 8:15; 9:25; Mark 6:5; 9:27; Luke 4:40). So it is also in two miracles instituted by our Lord, *miracles that continue to happen within the church today*—Holy Baptism and Holy Communion. In these miraculous divine actions, the Lord Jesus grants forgiveness of sins, life, and salvation by attaching His Word, His body, and His blood to water, bread, and wine—the common stuff of creation. In these, what do we receive but the gifts of everlasting healing? In these sacramental miracles, God continues to work as He has since the beginning.

The Sea-Dividing Staff

Briefly review what happened during the 10th plague (Exodus 12:29–32). After the Egyptians had let the Israelites go free, what thoughts filled their minds (Exodus 14:5)? How did they act on these thoughts (Exodus 14:6–9)?

After the 10th plague, Pharaoh was finally ready to throw in the towel. His firstborn son was dead, as were multitudes of others throughout the land of Egypt. Unshielded by the blood of the Passover lambs, these youths were slain by the destroying angel. Because of its leader's pigheadedness and its own maltreatment of Israel, the nation found itself casting dirt into the freshly dug graves of its offspring. While the Egyptians mourned, however, the chosen nation set its sights on the border of Egypt. They were free at last!

The Israelites didn't get far, however. Once again Pharaoh was breathing down their necks and snapping at their heels. You could almost have guessed it. Time and again, this leader had shown that his mouth held a forked tongue: he said "this" but really meant "that." Speaking out of both sides of his mouth was his greatest talent. Even though, on the horrific night of the 10th plague, he told Moses and Israel to get out, shortly thereafter, he and his servants second-guessed this decision. They asked, "What is this we have done, that we have let Israel go from serving us?" (Exodus 14:5). So off they went, six hundred chariots, filled with bloodthirsty warriors craving revenge. And there sat Israel, like a bird in a cage, camped beside the Red Sea.

When the Israelites saw the Egyptians coming, how did they react (Exodus 14:10–12)? What kind of heart did this reveal?

When the Israelites saw their former captors racing toward them, they panicked. Moses was to blame, they shrieked, for leading them out of slavery. With malicious intent, he had seduced them to leave their servitude, march into the desert, and meet a grim death there. Such is the voice of unbelief. Moses, however, like a shepherd trying to calm a flock of sheep surrounded by wolves, spoke to them: "Fear not, stand firm, and see the salvation of the LORD, which He will work for you today. For the Egyptians whom you see today, you shall never see again. The LORD will fight for you, and you have only to be silent" (Exodus 14:13–14).

What did the Lord tell Moses to do with the staff (Exodus 14:15–18)? What happened when he followed this Word of Yahweh (Exodus 14:21–22)?

Then it was God's turn to speak. To Moses He said:

> *"Why do you cry to Me? Tell the people of Israel to go forward. Lift up your staff, and stretch out your hand over the sea and divide it, that the people of Israel may go through the sea on dry ground. And I will harden the hearts of the Egyptians so that they shall go in after them, and I will get glory over Pharaoh and all his host, his chariots, and his horsemen. And the Egyptians shall know that I am the LORD, when I have gotten glory over Pharaoh, his chariots, and his horsemen." (Exodus 14:15–18)*

This would be the final round with Pharaoh. He had pushed God long enough. Again and again he had hardened his own heart; God in turn, by working against Pharaoh, had caused his heart to become even more hardened. This would be the leader's hour. He would go out—not with a bang but a splash.

But before punishment, there was salvation. Moses lifted the staff over the sea, as God had commanded, and a strong east wind blew all night, dividing the waters and drying the land. With "unmoistened foot," as one poet put it, the Israelites walked on the sea floor all night. They left the land of slavery behind, their eyes now set on the land of freedom graciously promised by the Lord.

Such a hope of divine favor had no place, however, in the hearts of Israel's enemies. They had declared war against God and were prepared, so it seemed, to fight to the death. What one might call the *11th* plague was about to befall Egypt. As with plagues one, two, three, seven, and eight, the staff of Moses would be the arm of Yahweh, by which He struck the enemy. Like the first plague, the turning of water into blood, so this plague would also turn water into blood, though in a different way. The Red Sea would be made crimson with the blood of Pharaoh and his soldiers, their bodies crushed by the cascading tonnage of waves.

When the princess of Egypt found Moses, she gave him a name which (in Hebrew) means "he who draws out." But how did the princess explain it (Exodus 2:10)? How was this name "prophetic" of what Moses would do now at the Red Sea?

Compare what Pharaoh did to the Israelites in Exodus 1:22 with what now happens at the Red Sea. How are these similar? What message does this convey?

It was time for payback. Long before, Pharaoh had issued the edict of infanticide, which decreed that every newborn Hebrew boy be cast into the Nile River. Now, as the proverb goes, "the chickens had come home to roost." And, irony of ironies, the man who would lift his staff to make it happen was, about 80 years earlier, the bawling baby boy who was lifted from a tiny floating basket by the princess of Egypt. She had named him Moses, saying, "Because I drew him out of the water" (Exodus 2:10). But the princess was not quite fluent in Hebrew; she got the grammar wrong. The name Moses (which, in Hebrew, is "Moshe") is indeed based on the root word which means "draw out," as in "draw out of water." But the name "Moshe" does not actually mean "I drew him out," like the daughter of Pharaoh said, but "he who draws out." The Lord, in his providence, was even using the not-so-accurate grammar of this princess to foretell, by the name of this baby boy, what a great act he would perform in his old age. For there stood that boy, now the famous leader of those emancipated slaves, *drawing out* of the water the people whom Pharaoh had so long confined. Moses "*mosesed*" the Israelites! Once placed in the Nile water by Pharaoh's word, he now led his people out of the Red Sea water by the Word of Yahweh. Then, once his people were safe, he sent that same water crashing down upon the tyrant. Everything was now reversed.

Read the "Song at the Sea" in Exodus 15. Compare the setting in which it is sung with Revelation 15:1–4. How are these two settings and songs similar? What is the overall theme of each song? Are the singers frightened or triumphant? Over what are they rejoicing? If their singing is prompted by the victory of Christ, that victory must in some way be parallel to the victory God gave Israel at the Red Sea. How are Christ's crucifixion and resurrection like the crossing of the sea and the destruction of the Egyptians?

When Israel stood on the non-Egyptian shore of the Red Sea, they "saw the Egyptians dead on the seashore" (Exodus 14:30). "They believed in the LORD and in His servant Moses" (Exodus 4:31). This faith, as a later psalm says, led to singing: "Then they *believed* His words; they *sang* His praise" (Psalm 106:12, emphasis added). Faith led to the hymn called the "Song at the Sea" or the "Song of Moses" (Exodus 15:1–18). Throughout all generations, this hymn has reverberated within the ears of the church, from the temple precincts in Jerusalem to Christian sanctuaries today.

This hymn of Moses, however, hearkened forward to another hymn as well. It set the tone for another song of victory and salvation, a song heard by St. John in the heavenly visions he recorded in

Revelation. Here is how the seer describes it:

> *Then I saw another sign in heaven, great and amazing, seven angels with seven plagues, which are the last, for with them the wrath of God is finished. And I saw what appeared to be a sea of glass mingled with fire—and also those who had conquered the beast and its image and the number of its name, standing beside the sea of glass with harps of God in their hands. And they sing the song of Moses, the servant of God, and the song of the Lamb, saying, "Great and amazing are Your deeds, O Lord God the Almighty! Just and true are Your ways, O King of the nations! Who will not fear, O Lord, and glorify Your name? For You alone are holy. All nations will come and worship You, for Your righteous acts have been revealed." (Revelation 15:1–4)*

Note well what is taking place. Divine wrath is finished. The plagues have all fallen. Around a sea of glass stand the victorious saints. This describes the church of Christ as she views with wonder and thanksgiving the work of the Messiah. But it paints this picture with the colors of the exodus and crossing of the Red Sea. As Israel once stood on the shore of the sea to behold the victory of Yahweh over the beastly Pharaoh, who had hounded the people of God all the way to this spot, so the new Israel shall stand on this sea. They shall see that the Pharaoh-like beast has lost. And they shall sing. With harps in their hands, they shall make glad music to the Lord, as Israel did so long ago. Joined with the believers of old, our voices shall mingle together as we sing both "the song of Moses, the servant of God, and the song of the Lamb." In poetic fusion, both testaments are brought together so that with one voice, the people of God harmoniously exalt His holy name and give thanks for all His benefits. For as God saved Israel at the Red Sea by means of a piece of wood, conquering that world power with such a common thing, so God has saved the world by means of a piece of wood, conquering the powers of darkness and sin upon the cross.

The Rock-Splitting Staff

Review what happens to the Israelites as they journey from the shores of the Red Sea to Mount Sinai (Exodus 15:22; 19:1). What kinds of struggles did they face? How did the people and Moses react?

Once the Israelites left the Red Sea, they headed for the mountain where God had appeared to Moses and to which He had told him to return once they left Egypt. The joy and faith that shone forth from the people when God vanquished the Egyptians faded quickly away. Most of their complaints originated from dry tongues and empty stomachs. First, there was no water, then only bitter water, until God sweetened the spring at Marah (Exodus 15:22–26). Then, they had no food, or at least not the kind of groceries or the amount they thought they needed. So God hushed their growling bellies and whining mouths with quail for meat and manna for bread (Exodus 16:1–36).

Read Exodus 17:1–7. What is Moses to do with the staff this time? How is this use of the staff similar to, but also radically different from, the way it was used in the 10 plagues? Compare this miracle especially with the first plague: how are they alike and how are they different?

Next, when they were very close to Mount Sinai, they again faced a lack of water. They were *not*, to be sure, in the midst of a Paradise with flowing streams. This place was not the land of a thousand lakes. The Sinai *wild*erness was indeed wild, a desert wasteland where water was scarce. Once again, they began to accuse Moses of national homicide, as if he had dragged them all out to the desert just so they could die of thirst. The accusation was foolish, of course, but people in dire straits often say very foolish things. In fact, they were so mad with thirst and rage that Moses thought his life was in jeopardy: "They are almost ready to stone me," he told the Lord (Exodus 17:4).

Yahweh, however, had the solution: "[He] said to Moses, 'Pass on before the people, taking with you some of the elders of Israel, and take in your hand the staff with which you struck the Nile, and go. Behold, I will stand before you there on the rock at Horeb, and you shall strike the rock, and water shall come out of it, and the people will drink.' And Moses did so, in the sight of the elders of Israel" (Exodus 17:5–6). He who turned the watery sea into dry land could turn a dry rock into a watery fountain. And so He did.

Once again, the staff is central to the miracle. The very same rod that served as the medium for divine wrath against Egypt was now the medium of divine goodness for Israel. This same double usage of the rod was noted in the Book of Wisdom of Solomon, a work that belongs to the collection of books known as the Apocrypha, written by Israelites in the centuries immediately prior to the birth of Christ. (The Roman Catholic Church considers the Book of Wisdom to be part of the Bible ["canonical"] while Lutherans echo Luther in regarding such literature as truly good and useful for Christians to read, but not inspired or authoritative for doctrine.) The author of Wisdom of Solomon says:

> *When [the Israelites] thirsted they called upon Thee, and water was given them out of flinty rock, and slaking of thirst from hard stone. For through the very things by which their enemies were punished, they themselves received benefit in their need. Instead of the fountain of an ever-flowing river, stirred up and defiled with blood in rebuke for the decree to slay the infants, Thou gavest them abundant water unexpectedly, showing by their thirst at that time how Thou didst punish their enemies. (Wisdom of Solomon 11:4–8 RSV)*

It is well worth reading those words more than once, for they are too rich and beautiful to catch the first time through. They point out that God gave His people water out of the "flinty rock," adding "for through the very things by which their enemies were punished, they themselves received benefit in their need." Through what things were the enemies punished? The rod and water. To rebuke Egypt for slaying Israelite infants, God "defiled with blood" the water of the Nile River with Moses' staff. To Israel in the desert, however, God did not give bloody water but "abundant water unexpectedly." Though He taught His own people a valuable lesson by letting them feel the pain of thirst—thereby showing them how He had punished their enemies—He soothed that pain by flooding the desert floor with water from the rock.

Who is standing on the rock Moses strikes? Read 1 Corinthians 10:1–4. Who does Paul say is the rock? How can this be? What does this tell us about Christ's presence in the Old Testament?

Though there are many fascinating questions to ask about this story, two must command our utmost attention: Who is on the rock? And what connection does this account have to the crucifixion of Jesus? First of all, the Lord Himself tells us who is on the rock—He is! "Behold, I will stand before you there at the rock at Horeb," He tells Moses (Exodus 17:6). But who exactly is this "Lord"? We have no need to guess even for a second, for St. Paul gives us the answer directly in his First Epistle to the Corinthians:

> *I want you to know, brothers, that our fathers were all under the cloud, and all passed through the sea, and all were baptized into Moses in the cloud and in the sea, and all ate the same spiritual food, and all drank the same spiritual drink.* For they drank from the spiritual Rock that followed them, and the Rock was Christ. *(1 Corinthians 10:1–4, emphasis added)*

Paul identifies the whole rock with none other than our Lord Jesus Christ. "The Rock was Christ," he affirms clearly and bluntly. This means that Christ Himself was the person of the Holy Trinity standing upon the rock; indeed, it means that Christ was the very source of the water. He was that Rock! Long before He was made flesh inside the Virgin Mary's womb, Christ was with His people. Indeed, from all eternity He is God. He is the one who appeared to Moses in the burning bush, was in the pillar of cloud and fire, and gave the Israelites drink "like the ocean depths," as the psalmist writes (78:15 NASB). He is the same yesterday, today, and forever: the Savior who is always near to those whom He loves.

Bearing in mind what happened with the rock in the wilderness and who stood atop it, read John 19:31–35. How might we read this event at the crucifixion in the light of what happened to the rock in the desert? What kind of drink do we receive from the Rock of our salvation?

Further clarification of the significance of this Christ-Rock is gained from a reflection upon the second question: What connection does this account have to the crucifixion of Jesus? In the Gospel of John, as the apostle describes what happened after the death but before the burial of Jesus, he says, "Since it was the day of Preparation, and so that the bodies would not remain on the cross on the Sabbath (for that Sabbath was a high day), the Jews asked Pilate that their legs might be broken and that they might be taken away. So the soldiers came and broke the legs of the first, and of the other who had been crucified with him. But when they came to Jesus and saw that He was already dead, they did not break His legs. But one of the soldiers pierced His side with a spear, and at once there came out blood and water. He who saw it has borne witness—his testimony is true, and he knows that he is telling the truth—that you also may believe" (19:31–35). The Rock of our salvation (Psalm 95:1) was pierced not with Moses' staff but a pagan soldier's spear; from the side of this Christ-Rock poured out blood and water. From ancient times, the church has related this blood to the Lord's Supper and the water to Baptism (AE 51:325). Out of the side of this Rock we find that which alone can and does satisfy our thirst. We drink His blood. We are washed in His holy water. We, like Israel, in the desert of our own sin, find relief in that which gushed forth when a piece of wood pierced the side of the Rock designated by God as the location of His presence.

The War Staff

Read Exodus 17:8–16. How is this staff used here? What is the staff called? When, earlier in the life of Moses, was this staff given the same name? Review what it means for the staff to be called this.

There is one more story about this rod of Israel's leader that occurs before Israel reaches Mount Sinai. While Israel was camped at a place called Rephidim, the Amalekites attacked (Exodus 17:8). Moses told Joshua (who is mentioned for the first time here) the plan of defense. He instructed him:

> *"Choose for us men, and go out and fight with Amalek. Tomorrow I will stand on the top of the hill with the staff of God in my hand." So Joshua did as Moses told him, and fought with Amalek, while Moses, Aaron, and Hur went up to the top of the hill. Whenever Moses held up his hand, Israel prevailed, and whenever he lowered his hand, Amalek prevailed. But Moses' hands grew weary, so they took a stone and put it under him, and he sat on it, while Aaron and Hur held up his hands, one on one side, and the other on the other side. So his hands were steady until the going down of the sun. And Joshua overwhelmed Amalek and his people with the sword. (Exodus 17:9–13)*

You can easily picture the scene. The fight is raging, Israel has the upper hand . . . when suddenly things begin to go from bad to worse. The lower Moses' hands sink, the lower Israel falls! So a commonsense solution is applied: put Aaron on one side and Hur on the other as human armrests. What a sight! Yet it works—it works wonderfully! Israel prevails under Joshua's leadership. The enemy attacks are squashed.

Picture Moses on the mountain with the staff. If the enemies of Israel had been told the day before this attack that they would be defeated because of the actions of a single man stretching out a common piece of wood in his wearied hands, how would they have reacted? How might we understand this victory by "foolish" means in the light of the cross? How do we see here a pattern of divine work?

But what is really going on? Why are the hands of Moses so important that unless they are lifted on high, his adversaries quickly begin to win? The answer is not the hands but what is in the hands. As Moses says: "I will stand on the top of the hill *with the staff of God in my hand.*" Outside of Exodus 4:20, which we discussed above, this is the only place in Scripture where the rod is explicitly named the "staff of God." But, as we have seen so many times, that is what it has been all along. The Word of the Lord has made it what it is—the divine instrument God chooses to use to bless His people.

Beginning already in the second century A.D., with the writings of a Christian named Justin Martyr, many preachers have likened the action of Moses stretching out his hands to that of our Lord upon the cross. Indeed, it is a comparison that, at the very least, shows a discernible pattern in the way our Savior chooses to redeem His people. Had the rough and tough Amalekites been told the day before the battle that Israel's victory depended upon the actions of a single man upon a hill stretching out a common piece of wood in his wearied hands, they would have laughed uncontrollably at such a childish, stupid notion. But, laugh as much as they would, that was the truth, and the next day, they knew it. So it was also with our Lord. Atop a hill, this lone man, His wearied hands stretched out upon the wood of the cross, must have looked like everything but a champion. But a champion He was and still is. Every enemy of hell was conquered; the foes of sin and death destroyed. Foolish and childish and stupid as it seems to the eyes of the "wise" world, that is how God accomplished salvation.

Conclusion

A simple piece of wood. That's all the staff of Moses was . . . until that day on Sinai when God made it His own. From that day onward, it was no longer just the dead remnant of a once-living tree. It had within it the powerful Word of God. This Word transformed the rod of Moses into the arm of the Lord, the means by which He could reach out either to clobber Egypt or caress Israel. Like so many other plain objects chosen by God to subdue His enemies—David's sling and Samson's donkey jawbone—the rod became a better weapon than any sword. But it was more than a weapon; it was an instrument of healing and salvation. It split the waters that Israel passed through; it opened up a fountain of water for the church. In that wood was life, the very life of our good and gracious God.

With such a noble history, it comes as no surprise that many fathers of the church—Lutheran fathers included—have likened the staff of Moses to the cross of Christ. For God chose both these common pieces of wood for a most uncommon work. When the hands of Moses grasped his rod and the hands of Jesus were nailed to the beam, something extraordinary was happening. The Lord of heaven and earth was acting for His people: defeating the foe, granting salvation, blessing His church with life. Thanks be to God for these plain pieces of wood by which He did for us what we could never, in a million lifetimes, have begun to do for ourselves.

Closing Prayer

Lord God, heavenly Father, as You once delivered Your people Israel by joining Your Word to the staff of Moses, so look with mercy upon Your people who are beset by temptations and sufferings in this world, and deliver them by Your means of grace; through Jesus Christ, our Lord. Amen.

THE STAFF OF MOSES

The Underdog

What are some biblical stories that come to mind in which the main character is an underdog? See, for example, **Judges 6–7** and **1 Samuel 17**. What kinds of odds do these people face? What are their enemies like?

What kinds of weapons are used by these underdogs? How would you characterize these weapons? See also the accounts in **Judges 3:31; 15:15**.

Why would God place weapons such as these in the hands of these underdogs? See **Psalm 44:6–7**.

What Is That in Your Hand?

Read **Exodus 3–4**. As God begins to outline His mission to Moses, how does Moses react? See **Exodus 3:11, 13; 4:1, 10, 13**.

How does God respond to Moses' question in **Exodus 4:1**? What message is sent by this miracle?

With what event is the serpent most closely associated in the Bible (**Genesis 3**)? Since this snake is transformed back into a staff by the hand of Moses, might this reversal (from something bad to something good) indicate something else that the Lord will soon reverse? How is the slavery in Egypt related to the work of the devil?

Read **Exodus 4:18–20**. Is this the same staff? Now to whom does the staff belong? What does this tell you about the purpose of the staff? Discuss other examples in Scripture in which the Lord claims something common, ordinary, and down-to-earth as His own? How is the "staff of God" related to these? What does this tell us about how God desires to work in this world?

The Snake Staff

Read **Exodus 5**. What kind of reception do Moses and Aaron receive from Pharaoh? How does Pharaoh respond to their request? How does Pharaoh set the other Israelites against Moses and Aaron?

Read **Exodus 7:1–13**. What does Aaron do with the staff? Why does he do it, that is, what message does this send to the Egyptians? What do the Egyptians do with their staffs? Are these two transformations exactly the same? How was the source behind the change in the rod of Aaron different from the source behind the change in the rods of the Egyptians? Why is this distinction all-important?

Compare the swallowing of the Egyptians' staffs with the later "swallowing" that took place at the Red Sea (**Exodus 15:10–12**). How was this incident in Pharaoh's palace a preview of what would later happen?

In what way did Pharaoh react to this event?

The Plaguing Staff

Read **Exodus 7:14–25**. How was the staff of Moses used in this first plague? How does Pharaoh react to this?

Read **Exodus 8:1–15**. How is this plague similar yet different from the first one? What purpose does the divine staff serve?

Read **Exodus 8:16–19**. What does Aaron do with the staff this time? What pattern has developed relative to the warning and inflicting of the plague? In what way is the reaction of the magicians different with regard to this plague?

In the fourth (flies), fifth (pestilence), and sixth (boils) plagues, no mention is made of the staff. But it is used again in the seventh (**Exodus 9:23**) and eighth plagues (**Exodus 10:12–13**). How would you characterize its use in each of these plagues? How else might God have brought down these plagues upon Egypt? That He did not merely speak His Word, but used a staff, informs us about how God works. What kinds of "staffs" might God use today to punish people or nations?

When Jesus performed miracles in the New Testament, they were not plagues. They were typically healings or some other kinds of blessings. What does this tell us about the purpose of our Lord's coming (see **John 3:16–17**)?

Moses had his staff—a created object—for these miracles of punishment. What kinds of created materials did Jesus use for His miracles of grace? See **John 9:6; Mark 8:5, 23; Matthew 14:13–21**.

What kinds of miracles take place every Lord's Day in the Divine Service? What created objects does Jesus use to perform these miracles?

The Sea-Dividing Staff

Briefly review what happened during the 10th plague (**Exodus 12:29–32**). After the Egyptians had let the Israelites go free, what thoughts filled their minds (**Exodus 14:5**)? How did they act on these thoughts (**Exodus 14:6–9**)?

When the Israelites saw the Egyptians coming, how did they react (**Exodus 14:10–12**)? What kind of heart did this reveal?

What did the Lord tell Moses to do with the staff (**Exodus 14:15–18**)? What happened when he followed this Word of Yahweh (**Exodus 14:21–22**)?

When the princess of Egypt found Moses, she gave him a name which (in Hebrew) means "he who draws out." But how did the princess explain it (**Exodus 2:10**)? How was this name "prophetic" of what Moses would do now at the Red Sea?

Compare what Pharaoh did to the Israelites in **Exodus 1:22** with what now happens at the Red Sea. How are these similar? What message does this convey?

Read the "Song at the Sea" in Exodus 15. Compare the setting in which it is sung with **Revelation 15:1–4**. How are these two settings and songs similar? What is the overall theme of each song? Are the singers frightened or triumphant? Over what are they rejoicing? If their singing is prompted by the victory of Christ, that victory must in some way be parallel to the victory God gave Israel at the Red Sea. How are Christ's crucifixion and resurrection like the crossing of the sea and the destruction of the Egyptians?

The Rock-Splitting Staff

Review what happens to the Israelites as they journey from the shores of the Red Sea to Mount Sinai (**Exodus 15:22; 19:1**). What kinds of struggles did they face? How did the people and Moses react?

Read **Exodus 17:1–7**. What is Moses to do with the staff this time? How is this use of the staff similar to, but also radically different from, the way it was used in the 10 plagues? Compare this miracle especially with the first plague: how are they alike and how are they different?

Who is standing on the rock Moses strikes? Read 1 **Corinthians 10:1–4**. Who does Paul say is the rock? How can this be? What does this tell us about Christ's presence in the Old Testament?

Bearing in mind what happened with the rock in the wilderness and who stood atop it, read **John 19:31–35**. How might we read this event at the crucifixion in the light of what happened to the rock in the desert? What kind of drink do we receive from the Rock of our salvation?

The War Staff

Read **Exodus 17:8–16**. How is this staff used here? What is the staff called? When, earlier in the life of Moses, was this staff given the same name? Review what it means for the staff to be called this.

Picture Moses on the mountain with the staff. If the enemies of Israel had been told the day before this attack that they would be defeated because of the actions of a single man stretching out a common piece of wood in his wearied hands, how would they have reacted? How might we understand this victory by "foolish" means in the light of the cross? How do we see here a pattern of divine work?

4

The Serpent Pole

Prayer

Lord God, heavenly Father, You provided healing for Your sinful people by raising up a bronze serpent upon a pole, that all who looked to it might live. You sent Your Son, Jesus Christ, that He might be lifted up onto the cross, that all who believe in Him may have eternal life. Lift up the eyes of our hearts to behold in faith Him who was crucified for us, that, trusting in Him, we may have the life that never ends; through the same, Jesus Christ, our Lord. Amen.

God: The Unconventional Physician

Discuss some rather off-the-wall remedies you have heard of. What makes them unconventional?

Years ago, a series of books entitled *Foxfire* was published. Each of the volumes centered around the old-style practices and traditions that were once followed by people in rural America, especially those on the farm or ranch. You can read about how your great-great-great-grandparents butchered hogs on the farm, raised their crops, trapped and hunted, built log barns, and a whole multitude of other interesting activities. As an added bonus, you can also read about how they cured their sicknesses, though—reader be warned—you will probably not want to imitate their procedures!

A great curiosity to many people today is how exactly certain cures or medicines were discovered. After all, how did these folks know that this bark or that root relieved a toothache? How did they come to find out that this leaf heals pinkeye while that mess of stuff (the contents of which you don't want to know), if swallowed, will relieve all the symptoms of gout? Truth be told, nobody really knows in most cases. The genesis of the medicine is hidden in the shadows of yesteryear.

Rather off-the-wall treatments for ailments are nothing uniquely American, of course. Every culture—civilized or not—has its own set of do-it-yourself remedies, some of which work, while others may very well endanger your life! Even those that have been well-tested and approved by the medical establishment are probably quite surprising when explained in layman's terms. What at first sounds outlandish, like it would never work, might turn out to be exactly what the doctor ordered.

Think of some biblical examples where God provided healing in rather unusual ways. For instance, see 2 Kings 5; 13:21; John 9:6; and Mark 8:23. What was the overall message sent by each of these miracles concerning the kind of "medicine" used by God?

The Bible has its fair share of unconventional remedies. Most of these are not prescribed by medical practitioners, but by the Lord and His prophets. For instance, when Naaman was infected with leprosy, he traveled from Syria to Israel to see "Dr. Elisha" (2 Kings 5), who instructed him to "go and wash in the Jordan seven times" to make his skin as new and fresh as an infant's. Though at first he balked at such a "silly" cure, Naaman was finally convinced, splashed on the water, and, sure enough, off came the leprosy. In the ministry of Jesus we see rather unusual treatments as well, such as when He healed a blind man with mud made from His own saliva (John 9:6–7) or when He spit on another man's eyes to heal them (Mark 8:23–25).

These rather odd methods of healing are not very odd, however, when viewed within the broader scheme of how our Lord works. Especially when we look at how He performs the miraculous, we see over and over how unusual His ways are to our human way of thinking. In our last lesson, for example, we studied how God chose a most bizarre weapon, the staff of Moses, to punish Egypt and rescue Israel. In this lesson we will direct our attention to another bizarre instrument of God. This instrument is not a weapon, but a source of healing. It is a pole, a tall wooden pole, erected within the camp of Israel. Attached to the top of this pole is a snake forged from bronze. We will observe, once more, how the Lord willed to use such common objects of wood and metal as conduits for divine blessings to His people.

Grumble, Grumble, Grumble

From the last lesson, where we studied the

staff of Moses, we have skipped forward almost 40 years. What led to 40 years of wandering in the wilderness (see Numbers 13–14)? What is the historical context of Numbers 21, that is, how close are they to the end of the 40 years? How should this have affected their outlook?

From our last lesson, we have skipped forward almost 40 years. When Moses struck the rock in the wilderness so that water gushed out to quench the thirst of the Israelites, and when he raised his staff so that Amalek was defeated, the nation had just left Egypt about three months prior. After these incidents, they camped at Mount Sinai, where they remained for about a year. There the Lord gave them the Ten Commandments, they built the tabernacle, and they prepared for their journey to the Promised Land. The future looked sweet.

When they arrived at the border of Canaan, however, everything quickly soured (Numbers 13–14). Of the dozen scouts whom Moses sent to scope out the land, only two (Joshua and Caleb) encouraged the people to enter the country, battle the inhabitants, and claim what God had promised to give them. The rest of the scouts said that, yes, the land was flowing with milk and honey, but if they attacked, it would soon be flowing with their lifeblood as well! They also claimed that beside the huge citizens of Canaan, the Israelites would look like grasshoppers, ready to be smashed. "There's no way we can do it," they said.

Sadly, the nation had ears only for the bad news from these 10 killjoy scouts, not the encouraging reports of Caleb and Joshua. They whined, they murmured, they rebelled. In fact, they came very close to stoning Moses and Aaron! Such rank unbelief, coupled with such hatred and violence, unleashed the wrath of God. He swore that this generation would never enter the Promised Land; their corpses would litter the desert sands. And so it was. "For forty years I loathed that generation," God later said (Psalm 95:10). For four decades this loathed people wandered in the wilderness region. It was a slow, painful death for one generation in Israel. Toward the end even the members of Moses' famous family began to die: first his sister, Miriam (Numbers 20:1); then his older brother, Aaron (20:22–29). Now only Moses was left, and his 120 years were quickly drawing to a close.

What happened to the Israelites in Numbers 21:1–3? What impact would this have had on national morale? How might it also have led to problems such as pride?

At the beginning of Numbers 21, things were looking a little better. After being attacked by the Canaanite king Arad, then winning a decisive victory against him, the nation must have been pleased. Perhaps this would be the turning point for them. The 40 years of punishment were nearly over; the land God had sworn to give to Abraham, Isaac, Jacob, and their offspring was virtually at their fingertips.

In Numbers 21:4, the people are going "around the land of Edom." Why? (See Numbers 20:14–21.) What is the relationship between Israel and the Edomites? Think back to their "founders," Jacob and Esau. Look in a Bible atlas to trace the roundabout route the Israelites were forced to take. What kind of impact did this have on the nation (Numbers 21:4–5)?

Rather than attacking from the south, the Israelites took a roundabout route. They would travel to the eastern side of the Jordan River and move in from there. To get to that location, however, they had to go through a narrow strip of land belonging to Edom. This group of people was what one might call a "brother nation" to Israel. The Edomites were the descendants of Esau, while the Israelites were from the line of Esau's brother, Jacob. These two siblings, however, almost always had a rocky relationship: Esau sold his birthright to Jacob for a bowl of lentil soup (Genesis 25:29–34); Jacob deceived his father, Isaac, into giving the blessing of the firstborn to him instead of to his older brother (27:1–29); when Esau discovered his younger brother's trickery, he planned a revenge killing (27:30–41); then Jacob fled for his life (27:42–28:5). Theirs was not exactly one big happy family. Though there was reconciliation in later years between the brothers, the history of the nations descended from them—Israel and Edom—was almost continually marked by turbulence and violence.

Thus in Numbers 20:14–21, when Israel requested permission to pass through the land of Edom on their way to the Promised Land, the king refused. Even though the people of Israel offered to keep to the highway, to avoid damaging all fields and vineyards, and even to pay for the water they drank, Edom still answered in the negative. In fact, the Edomite army even came out with a show of force to underline their rejection of the fraternal request. Not wanting a fight, Israel was forced to choose another way.

This other way turned out to be one major headache. "From Mount Hor, they set out by the way to the Red Sea, to go around the land of Edom" (Numbers 21:4). This "Red Sea" is not the Red Sea next to Egypt, which Moses divided with his staff, but the body of water more commonly called the Gulf of Aqabah on the western border of modern-day Saudi Arabia. A quick glance at the map on the student page shows what an out-of-the-way trip this turned out to be. And not only was it a huge inconvenience with regard to the sheer length; the deserts through which they passed were a veritable haven of all kinds of unpleasantries, not the least of which were several kinds of venomous serpents. We'll hear more about them in a moment.

Look at verse 5 carefully. Against whom do the Israelites complain? The Hebrew word for "you" in "why have *you* brought us up" is plural. Compare this with the similar complaint of their fathers' generation in Exodus 17:3 (where the "you" is singular). Which is the stronger complaint? What kind of twisted image of God do they describe? What indication does this give about how much the children are walking in the footsteps of their fathers?

So how did the Israelites react to this circuitous route? About the same way a four-year-old, strapped in his car seat with a sweater on, would react to a 12-hour summer trip in a car with no air-conditioning! You get the picture. Moses writes, "The people became impatient on the way" (Numbers 21:4). In Hebrew this phrase is more vivid: "The soul of the people grew short in the way." This was way more than these "short-souled" travelers were willing to stomach, so bellyaching began in earnest: "The people spoke against God and against Moses, 'Why have you brought us up out of Egypt to die in the wilderness? For there is no food and no water, and we loathe this worthless food' " (Numbers 21:5). These words ought to sound hauntingly familiar, for virtually this same complaint was muttered by the fathers and mothers of this generation not long after they had exited the land of slavery (Exodus 17:1–3). Less than three months after they all had seen the amazing miracle at the Red Sea, had believed in the Lord and Moses, and had burst out in praise for His gracious action—yes, *less than three months later*—all they could think about was themselves, their thirst, their woe-is-me situation. They were camped at Rephidim, where there was no water for the people to drink, so they whined accusingly, "Why did you bring us up out of Egypt, to kill us and our children and our livestock with thirst?" (Exodus 17:3). "Why did you bring us up out of Egypt?" So said the fathers at the beginning of the 40 years and so said their sons at the end. The apple had not fallen far from the tree, and rotten was the fruit.

In fact, at least in their complaining, the sons were even worse than their parents! The moms and dads only quarreled with Moses, asking, "Why have you [singular] brought us up?" Hateful as their words were, at least they wag their accusatory fingers at Moses alone. The next generation, however, goes further in Numbers 21:5: "Why have you [plural] brought us up out of Egypt to die in the wilderness?" Now they are expressly blaming Moses *and God* for their predicament. Never mind the fact that they have been told repeatedly that Yahweh used Moses to free them from slavery because He loves them; never mind the fact that if God had wanted them all in the grave He could have snapped His fingers and accomplished that; never mind the fact that He had stood by their side for four long decades despite their incessant bawling about this or that burden they must bear—yes, never mind all that. They know better. They know that God is really a tightfisted, mean-spirited tyrant who had just been toying with them these last 40 years, like a cat with a mouse.

What two contradictory things do the Israelites say about food in Numbers 21:5? What is the real problem with regard to food?

Not content, however, to stop with such an acidic question, they press further: "For there is no food and no water, and we loathe this worthless food" (Numbers 21:5). Wait a minute! Is there food or is there not food? They claim "there is no food" yet also complain "we loathe this miserable food." Aha! They've been trapped in their own lie. They sound just like boys and girls who are standing in front of a refrigerator, the door open wide, food nearly spilling out of it onto the floor, bellowing, "Mom, Dad, there's nothing to eat!" No, there's plenty to eat. The problem is not need but want. Like the children before the refrigerator, the Israelites had plenty to eat—God had been giving them manna the whole time they had been in the wilderness—but they did not have what they wanted. They hankered after something sweeter and better, and thus loathed that "worthless food" God had rained down from above. But *turning up* their noses at food which elsewhere is called the "bread from heaven" (Psalm 105:40) was but an outward symptom of the fact that they were completely *turned in* on themselves. They despised the gifts of God, pushing them away like spinach or, worse yet, scraps fit only for swine.

How is the incident described in John 6:1–15 and 22–51 like this one in the wilderness? Look especially at verses 41–43. About what was Jesus' audience grumbling? Both in Numbers and John, what did the people not trust? How are we the same way? How do we treat the gifts of God in creation? How do we treat the gifts of God in the church? How do we show our lack of trust? Give examples.

This grumbling of the Israelites concerning food and drink, a grumbling that began with their fathers and continued with the next generation, was not quickly silenced. In fact, 14 hundred years later, its echoes were still heard. After our Lord Jesus fed over 5,000 people with only five barley loaves and two fish, He left the crowds and crossed the Sea of Galilee, walking atop the water for part of the way (John 6:1–21). Happy with their full bellies, the multitudes scampered after Him, racing round the lake to meet Him on the opposite shore. They had every intent of crowning Him—as is often said—their "Bread King." This is what He Himself accused them of: "Truly, truly, I say to you, you are seeking Me, not because you saw signs, *but because you ate your fill of the loaves*" (John 6:26, emphasis added). Soon thereafter, Jesus launches into a sermon about the manna in the wilderness (John 6:32–58). In this homily, He proclaims that He is the "true bread from heaven" (John 6:32); the "bread of life" (John 6:35); the "bread of God . . . who comes down from heaven and gives life to the world" (John 6:33). Then, like their forefathers, the crowd began to complain: "The Jews grumbled about Him, because He said, 'I am the bread that came down from heaven'" (John 6:41). In the original Greek text of John's Gospel, the word used to describe the grumbling of the Jews is the same word used in the Greek translation of Exodus and Numbers to describe the grumbling of the Israelites. The connection is painfully obvious. Just as their fathers of old had complained about a lack of food *precisely because they doubted the Word of the Lord* that promised He would provide, so the Jews who listened to Jesus grumbled because they rejected His Word. In both cases, the language of grumbling was the language of unbelief. As they had despised the manna from above, so now they despised the true Manna, the Bread of Life, who had come down from His Father to give life to them and to the world.

The unpleasant truth is that such an attitude is universal among fallen humanity. We are just as guilty as they were. Blatantly, incessantly, we treat the gifts of God with contempt. Our food is not tasty enough; our clothing is not stylish enough; our bodies are not beautiful enough; our families are not as understanding as they should be; our jobs are not as fulfilling as they ought to be; our paycheck is not as fat as we want it to be; our church is not as loving as we think it should be. The grumbling goes on and on.

But more serious still is how we treat the gifts of salvation in the same way. The Word of the Lord is not as exciting as we would have it be; the pastor's preaching is not as inspiring as we desire; the service takes too long if we have Communion every Sunday; these hymns are not entertaining enough; these prayers don't have the vitality they should have. Here also, on and on it goes. He who claims to be without sin in this regard, as well as he who claims to have *little sin* in this regard, only lies to himself and God. We are Israelites to the core. The bawling with which we fill the room upon leaving our mothers' wombs is rarely set aside for humble, heartfelt giving of thanks for all the undeserved benefits daily heaped upon us. From the cradle to the coffin our mother tongue is complaining with a capital *C*.

For that reason, we ought to pay careful heed to the rest of this story, both for what it teaches about the anger and the love of the Lord God of Israel.

Fiery Serpents

What did the Lord do in response to the people's complaints (Numbers 21:6)? What kind of snakes were these? Why were they called "fiery" serpents?

Into the midst of this camp of grumbling desert travelers came a serpentine surprise, and not just one. This, however, was not an accidental snake stampede. God appointed these reptiles as His agents of divine wrath: "The LORD sent fiery serpents among the people, and they bit the people, so that many people of Israel died" (Numbers 21:6). Slithering into their midst were divinely commissioned executors of justice. They were armed to the teeth, quite literally. When their fangs entered Israelite flesh, the mark they left was the stamp of divine *dis*approval. God was unhappy, and with good reason. His own people had become just as bad as—if not worse than—Pharaoh, from whose iron grip God had released them. As Pharaoh had hardened his heart to the Word and work of Yahweh, the Israelites had now done the same. However, they of all people should have known better. So now the tables were turned; Israel was being plagued, not Egypt.

Biblical scholars dispute the identifying characteristic of these "fiery serpents." Why were they called "fiery"? Was it because they had a fiery glow about them? Were they firelike in color? Or did it have to do with the inflammation caused by their bites? Although complete certainty is lacking, most side with the last explanation—that their venomous bites burned like fire. Whatever the reason for their name, the result of their attacks is beyond question: "many people of Israel died." That is where unbelief and rebellion always lead in the end: to the grave. "The wages of sin is death," teaches St. Paul (Romans 6:23). And the sinner's paycheck is always paid in full.

The Bible speaks of three kinds of death. Look up these verses and describe each kind of death; note also if such a death is universal or if it only befalls some people: (a) Ephesians 2:1–3; (b) Genesis 5; (c) Revelation 2:11; 20:6, 14–15; 21:8.

It would be helpful at this time to remember that the Scriptures speak of three kinds of death. Although these are closely intertwined, they are still to be distinguished, for not every person suffers all three kinds of death. First, there is *spiritual death*. This is the kind of death St. Paul is speaking of when he writes to the Christians in Ephesus, "You were dead in the trespasses and sins in which you once walked, following the course of this world, following the prince of the power of the air, the spirit that is now at work in the sons of disobedience" (Ephesians 2:1–3). All people are conceived and born in this sin-death. Thus every child who leaves the womb is a *spiritual stillborn*, in need of rebirth and life in Holy Baptism.

The second kind of death is *physical death*. Of all the people who have ever lived, only Enoch

(Genesis 5:24) and Elijah (2 Kings 2:9–12) were spared this bodily demise. It is inescapable, both for unbelievers and believers. For believers, however, physical death is not master but slave, for it "serves" the believer by freeing him from existence in this world of sin that he might enter his heavenly homeland. Such a death is never good—it is still a result of sin—but it is an evil that is used by God for a good purpose. For unbelievers, on the other hand, death of the body leads only to a far worse death.

This death is *everlasting death* in hell. Though third on our list, it is what Revelation calls the "second death" (2:11; 20:6, 14–15; 21:8), to be distinguished from the first death, which is physical. St. John writes, "Death and Hades were thrown into the lake of fire. This is the *second death*, the lake of fire. And if anyone's name was not found written in the book of life, he was thrown into the lake of fire" (Revelation 20:14–15, emphasis added). To be written in the book of life is, quite simply, to be *in Christ*, who is the Book of Life—to believe in Him and be baptized into His body. Those bathed in the fountain of His baptismal love will not be drowned in the lake of fire.

What kind(s) of death did the Israelites experience in the desert?

Returning now to the story of Israel in the wilderness, we might ask: What kind of death did these Israelites experience who were bitten by the fiery serpents? We must say, first of all, that it was *spiritual death* that caused the judgment to fall upon the camp. That is not to say that the camp was filled with nothing but unbelievers. After all, even believers are still partly unbelievers while in this world. What St. Paul terms the "old man" (Colossians 3:9 KJV), the sinful nature, still remains incorrigible, unbelieving, unyielding to God's Word, even in the Christian. That is why, as the Small Catechism teaches, the "Old Adam in us should by daily contrition and repentance be drowned and die with all sins and evil desires, and . . . a new man should daily emerge and arise to live before God in righteousness and purity forever." This spiritually dead "Old Adam" within the Israelites raised his ugly head to murmur and complain against God's good gifts, leading to the outbreak of serpents and the ensuing *physical death*.

What about *everlasting death*? When the snakes sank their fangs into Israelite flesh, did souls begin to sink into hell with nothing to stop them? Did the fiery bite lead inexorably to a fiery hell? That the serpents' venom led not only to death of the body but also death forever in the lake of fire is certainly possible. And, probably, at least in the case of some of those who were bitten, that did sadly happen. There was also, however, a chance for repentance and faith.

And that takes us to the next part of the story.

Repentance and Intercession

Psalm 78 is a poem that recalls the exodus. It records not only God's loving deeds, but also the rebellious deeds of the Israelites. In verses 32–34, what does the author say finally brought the people to repentance? What is it about death that finally brings some people to the point of confession?

The Psalms include several hymns that recount the basic story of the exodus and wilderness wanderings (e.g., Psalms 78, 105, 106, 135, 136). In one of these, Psalm 78, a major theme is the rebellion of Israel in the desert. Many of the major episodes of Israelite murmuring are cited, along with the divine anger that followed them. As if throwing up his hands in disgust and impatience, the author, Asaph, says: "In spite of all this, they still sinned; despite His wonders, they did not believe. So He made their days vanish like a breath, and their years in terror. *When He killed them, they sought Him*; they repented and sought God earnestly" (Psalm 78:32–34, emphasis added). These few words, "when He killed them, [then] they sought him," are some of the best in Holy Scripture to describe what it often takes to bring hard-hearted people back to God. When He warned them through Moses, they yawned; when He chastened them through hunger and thirst, they bellyached; even when He killed some select rebels among the people, they only grumbled more. But when He killed them, when His wrath fell not upon a few but many, then and only then did they seek Him. Nothing helps us focus more clearly on life than death. It helps to clear away delusions of our own grandeur, it makes us ask questions we otherwise rarely ask, and it points our eyes toward what is beyond this life. It is, in many respects, a slap in the face to shock us back from our self-created virtual realities into the one true reality—God Himself.

"When He killed them, they sought Him." The psalmist does not tell us whether or not he had in mind the Israelite deaths from venomous snakes, but his words would surely apply to that situation. For when God killed many of them, the survivors took notice. Like the prodigal son in Jesus' parable, who "came to himself" while surrounded by the pigs (Luke 15:17), so the Israelites *came to themselves*—came to their spiritual senses—when surrounded by the serpents. And if the lowliness of the pigs signified the lowliness of the prodigal, then the serpents signified that the people of Israel had gone the way of the hellish serpent; they had been deceived by the fallen angel who tempted their parents in times past.

Read the confession of the Israelites (Numbers 21:7). Is it complete? Do they speak truthfully? In what way is confession saying "Amen" back to God?

When they came to themselves, they sought divine absolution and healing: "The people came to Moses and said, 'We have sinned, for we have spoken against the LORD and against you. Pray to the LORD, that He take away the serpents from us' " (Numbers 21:7). There is hardly a better confession than that uttered in the first part of the people's response. Biblically speaking, to confess is *to say the same thing as God*, to echo back to the Lord what He first says to us. Thus as "the people spoke against God and against Moses" (Numbers 21:5), so they confess "we have spoken against the LORD and against you" (Numbers 21:7). They say "Amen" to what the Scriptures record: "It is true. We have sinned."

This is the pattern of confession in the church as well. Sinners have no need of either exaggerating their sins or of downplaying their seriousness. They have no need of making up or masking sins, explaining the motives or reasons behind this or that transgression. They are simply to say "Amen" to what the Lord has already said about them. "If we say we have not sinned, we make [God] a liar" (1 John 1:10), for He has spoken the truth about us. We are the liars, liars who only speak the truth when we say, "I am a liar." Yes, sinners can say hardly anything more truthful than when they confess, "I have sinned. God is right. Amen."

Why do the Israelites go to Moses and ask him to intercede? Why did they not pray for themselves? See Exodus 32:11–14; Numbers 11:1–3; Numbers 14:13–19. How is Moses like Jesus in this respect (Romans 8:34)?

After the Israelites' confession, they proceed to ask Moses to pray for them. This request is good and right, inasmuch as Moses had been and still was a mediator for the people. He interceded for them when they built the golden calf (Exodus 32:11–14), when fire burned up some complainers at Taberah (Numbers 11:1–3), when they refused to enter the Promised Land (Numbers 14:13–19), and other times as well. As a figure like Christ, Moses stood between the Lord's wrath and the nation so deserving of that wrath and prayed that God would have mercy. As the Son of God prayed for us while visibly on earth (e.g., John 17) and indeed still intercedes for us in heaven (Romans 8:34), so Moses prayed for Israel.

What exactly did the Israelites ask Moses to pray for? What did they want God to do? Did He give them their request or something better? Do we always pray for what we truly need? How does God answer prayers such as these?

As is often the case with the prayers of sinners, however, what they prayed for was not exactly what they needed. They wanted God to take away the serpents from them. Note that there is absolutely nothing wrong with such a request. It is the virtual equivalent of an ill person praying that God would take away the sickness afflicting him. Even though the Lord did not give them exactly what they prayed for, He was certainly pleased with their request. That is His way. He does not demand that we pray perfectly, that is, always asking only and exactly what we should. As St. Paul tell us, "We do not know what to pray for as we ought" (Romans 8:26). That is to say, very often in our prayers we are like children who ask their parents for things that are really not the best for them. But loving and wise mothers and fathers do not always give their children precisely what they ask for, but always strive to give what is truly the best for them. So our heavenly Father always grants us those gifts that are for our good, for the good of our life here and our life in heaven.

The Lord of all wisdom knew what was best for His people who were suffering under the penalty of the snakes. He did not take away the serpents; or, if He did, we are not told that He did. Instead, He provided something better. That "something better" brings us to the climax of the story.

The Bronze Serpent

After Moses prayed, the Lord said to him, " 'Make a fiery serpent and set it on a pole, and everyone who is bitten, when he sees it, shall live.' So Moses made a bronze serpent and set it on a pole. And if a serpent bit anyone, he would look at the bronze serpent and live" (Numbers 21:8–9).

Imagine what the Israelites must have thought when Moses made the bronze serpent. To what might we compare this? It would be like a gunshot victim told to look at a ______. Like a cancer patient told to look at a ________. Give other examples. Recall Genesis 3. How would this story have affected their view of the bronze serpent?

Pause a minute, if you will, to ponder just how strange this must have seemed to the Israelites. There, on the pole, was the very likeness of what afflicted them! It would be like God telling a cancer patient to gaze at a portrait of the tumor inside him, like a gunshot victim told to stare into the face of the one who pulled the trigger. If we were to have speculated about what God might do, we might suspect He would appear in the pillar of fire and have them look to that for healing. Or, we might expect Him to direct Moses to some plant or herb that was endowed with miraculous power to heal the snakebites. Anything but this snake on a pole!

What's more, in Israel, the serpent was inseparably bound to the story of the fall. This was Satan's disguise, the emblem of sin and death and all that is anti-God. Shall they look to that which cannot but bring to their remembrance the origin of all that is evil in the world? Yes, they shall, for there is healing nowhere else. Truly, there is no more bizarre cure in all Scripture than this one.

Yet it worked, of course, as the Word of the Lord said it would. Moses crafted the bronze serpent so that it looked like one of the fiery serpents. He attached it to a wooden pole and raised it up. If anyone in the camp of Israel was bitten and looked at the bronze serpent, the venom in them would be as harmless as water.

As bizarre as this cure was to human eyes, there was divine wisdom in this choice. Discuss the following: The Lord not only sent the punishment, but He also provided the cure. What does this tell us about the justice and mercy of our God? What was the bronze serpent a graphic reminder of? What did the Israelites have to "do" to be healed? What does this tell us about how God provides salvation? Compare with Romans 6:8–9. Why did God use a symbol that would have appeared foolish in the eyes of the world? Compare with 1 Corinthians 1:18–31.

As weird as this cure seems at first glance, upon further reflection there is something wondrously wise revealed here. First of all, both the sickness and the cure arise from the same source—the Lord God of Israel. As "the LORD sent fiery serpents among the people" (Numbers 21:6), so He also sent Moses to "make a fiery serpent and set it on a pole" (Numbers 21:8). "The LORD kills and brings to life," as Hannah sings (1 Samuel 2:6). He does both, for life and death and all things are in His hands. He could very well have ignored the prayer of Israel and Moses. He could have let the serpents bite and bite and bite until the camp was nothing but corpses. In other words, He could have acted *fairly*—given them what justice demanded—but instead He acted graciously. Thank God He is not fair but merciful! He did not exhaust His wrath upon them. He who is love acted in conformity with His nature. He healed. He enlivened. He had compassion.

Second, it was good that their cure was an emblem of their malady, for, while God provided healing through it, He also used it to remind them of the source of their pain—sin itself. Externally, the snake on the pole was not a pretty sight. It was ugly, as ugly as iniquity is. There is no need to shy away from the bitter truth. The fangs of Satan that had pierced the heart and soul of Adam and Eve had pierced the Israelites as well. The poison of original sin ran through their veins. This metal reptile on the pole was a graphic reminder of that truth.

Third, this sign of healing reveals the will of God that man be saved by faith alone, not by good works. This cure was so incredibly simple as to be truly *incredible*—that is—not believable. You can almost hear the first reaction of the Israelites: "What! Cured by that horrid thing!" But God says, "Yes. That's it. Look, believe, and you shall be healed. There are no strings attached. No fine print. No additional charges. I give you healing completely free of charge. There it is. Believe Me. I love you." No work was required of them. No reparations needed to be made. God Himself provided the means of healing, the invitation to believe, and even the gift of faith itself. It was all His doing.

Fourth, in conformity with His work elsewhere, this sign is *to the eyes of the world* utterly foolish. We have underlined this point elsewhere many times because it is of such supreme importance in the Christian life. God cannot be found and will not be found where human reason thinks He is. He makes foolish the wisdom of the world. He acts in ways unexpected by mankind. He uses the lowly and despised and that which seems contrary to His nature. After all, here is God's healing power bound up in the icon of Satan. That is unthinkable unless thought about with the mind of Christ.

Read John 3:1–17 (especially v. 14) in light of Numbers 21. Discuss the following questions: Here Jesus compares Himself to a serpent. How could such a lowly animal accurately represent Jesus? See Isaiah 52:13–53:12. Why would Jesus liken Himself to something that hearkens back to Satan in Genesis 3? Why does the Messiah embody Satan's work of evil in this world in order to atone for that evil (2 Corinthians 5:21)?

How are we in a similar situation to the Israelites, yes, an even worse situation? To what are we to look? Some would say we are to look to the "cross," but how can we see the cross now? How is the cross made "visible" today? The Israelites who looked to the bronze serpent were healed; what does Jesus say we who believe in Him receive? After this lesson and other lessons in this study, in what ways can you now better appreciate and affirm what Luther says about the relationship of Christ to this story? How has this opened up the Scriptures for you?

Lastly, and most importantly, something is revealed here that goes beyond what is recorded in Numbers 21. During our Lord's conversation with Nicodemus (John 3), right before some of the most well-known words of the Bible, Jesus refers to this incident in the life of Israel. He says, "As Moses lifted up the serpent in the wilderness, so must the Son of Man be lifted up, that whoever believes in Him may have eternal life. For God so loved the world, that He gave His only Son, that whoever believes in Him should not perish but have eternal life" (John 3:14–16).

Now this is a most amazing comparison: Christ compared to a serpent! In fact, Martin Luther probably speaks for most of us when he says, "Who would have had the boldness to refer this story to Christ? I would never have ventured to interpret this story as Christ Himself did when He plainly related it to Himself" (AE 22:339). Yet there is the comparison, right from the lips of Jesus. But the questions arise: How is our Lord like the bronze serpent? How is His cross like the pole erected by Moses? How is believing in Him similar to looking at the snake placed on the pole?

As mentioned before, the bronze serpent was connected not only with the serpents that slithered into the camp of Israel, but was also reminiscent of the satanic snake that slithered into Eden. It was impossible to think of one without thinking of the other. So when Jesus directly links Himself and His coming execution with the bronze serpent, He places Himself within the orbit of these stories as well. We must think of Him, as Luther says, as "our *Serpent of salvation*, symbolized for us by that earlier bronze serpent" (AE 22:340). Christ is our Serpent of salvation, Luther goes on to say, because "God would let His Son descend from heaven and be nailed to the cross, where He, too, hangs like a serpent or a worm, the object of scorn and contempt, as Christ Himself laments in Psalm 22:6" (AE 22:340). In this lamentation in Psalm 22:6, David, foreshadowing the Messiah, prays, "But I am a worm and not a man, scorned by mankind and despised by the people." Be He called a serpent or worm, both indicate His despised condition as the Suffering Servant. Isaiah prophesies that the Messiah will be surrounded by sin and sinners in His death: "He was despised and rejected by men; a man of sorrows, and acquainted with grief; and as one from whom men hide their faces He was despised, and we esteemed Him not" (53:3); "the LORD has laid on Him the iniquity of us all" (53:6); "He . . . was numbered with the transgressors" (53:12). The Old Testament itself thus prophesies that the Messiah will not end His life surrounded by earthly glory and fame but rather by suffering, pain, and ignominy. Therefore, when Christ compares Himself to the serpent, there is certainly a precedent for this in the Psalms and Prophets of Israel.

But how can we so closely connect Christ to Satan, the hellish serpent of Eden? Are these two not diametrically opposed? Yes, they are opposed to one another. What Christ does, however, is willingly to take upon Himself the result of all Satan's work. Though pure and holy in Himself, He becomes our impurity and our unholiness on the cross that He might do away with them by His atoning death. Paul puts it this way: "For our sake [God] made Him to be sin who knew no sin, so that in Him we might become the righteousness of God" (2 Corinthians 5:21). Though Jesus had no sin of His own, He became sin. He became the world's sin. He became all that Satan had striven so hard to create on earth. He became the Sinner so that when God poured out His wrath upon Him, that wrath might be totally spent.

Thus, on the cross we see our Serpent of salvation, the very Holy One of God who became like Satan that He might defeat Satan. Atop that piece of wood hung the world's sin, death, and punishment, all compacted within His flesh and bones. Now we are directed to look to Him to be saved. He is lifted up "that whoever believes in Him may have eternal life" (John 3:15). The Israelites lifted up their eyes and looked to the bronze serpent, which had God's Word attached to it, and were saved from physical death. We too have had the venomous poison of Satan injected into our bodies and souls. We too are subject to death. There is no escape from this except through the One who is lifted up on the wood of the cross. To look to Him is to believe in Him, to trust in His Word, to know that He is our healer. That is how God loved the world. He gave His only Son to be our Serpent of salvation that whoever believes in Him should not perish from the venomous bite of the devil but have eternal life in the promised land above.

Oh, the mysterious ways of God! Who would have ever thought that God would use a serpent as a symbol of salvation? This was hidden from all human reason. It is revealed only to those who *see through their ears*, that is, who see what God speaks, who give heed not to what their eyes tell them but to what their ears hear from the divine mouth.

In conclusion, one more noteworthy aspect of this story is that it teaches us how to read the Old Testament with Christ always before our eyes. As Luther said in the quote above, had Christ not made this comparison explicit, who would have had the boldness to refer this story to Jesus? But our Lord does, and in so doing He teaches us how we are to read biblical stories such as these. Listen to these insightful words from Luther. They are worth remembering when reading the Old Testament:

> *In this way the Lord shows us the proper method of interpreting Moses and all the prophets.* He teaches us that Moses points and refers to Christ in all his stories and illustrations. *His purpose is to show that Christ is the point at the center of a circle, with all eyes inside the circle focused on Him. Whoever turns his eyes on Him finds his proper place in the circle of which Christ is the center.* All the stories of Holy Writ, if viewed aright, point to Christ.
>
> *During the forty days between Christ's resurrection and His ascension He expounded many similar texts and related many such stories to His disciples in His conversations with them (Luke 24:27). He did the same thing when He appeared on Mt. Tabor with Moses and Elijah (Matthew 17:3). Thus He also relates the figure of the serpent to Himself here. Thereby He opens the treasure chest of Moses and shows them the nugget concealed there.* He shows that all the stories and illustrations of Moses point to Christ. *The precious treasure of looking solely at Christ was so near and dear to Moses that he wore it, so to speak, between his skin and his flesh.* (AE *22:339–340, emphasis added)*

For Luther, all the Old Testament is about Jesus, not just a prophecy here or there. This is the case here as well. In the story of the serpent on the pole, we see Jesus prefigured.

Conclusion

What a diversity we see in God's use of wood in the Holy Scriptures! There were the two trees in Eden, the burning bush, the staff of Moses, and now the pole for the serpent. Yet beneath this diversity is commonality, for all of them are instruments in the hand of God to work good for His people. To each one of them God connected His Word of grace. Through each one of them God gave what His people needed.

On the pole of wood in the desert hung a most unusual cure for snakebite—the image of a snake. Yet the image conveyed a real healing, for it had within it the promise of God's Word. Whoever looked to that bronze serpent lived. This is also the case with the wood upon which our Serpent of salvation hung. Those who look to Him are cured not of a common snakebite but of the bite of sin, death, and the devil. He who became our sin—who became our Serpent—takes it away from us that we might have in exchange His righteousness. In Him we are healed forever.

Closing Prayer

If some lust in current fashion
Rises like a fi'ry flood,
Draw me to Your cross and Passion,
Quench the fire, Lord, by Your blood.
Lest I to the tempter yield,
Let me front him with the shield,
Thorn-crowned, blood-marked tree displaying,
Sign the devils find dismaying.

("Grant, Lord Jesus, that My Healing," *LW* 95:2)

The Serpent Pole

God: The Unconventional Physician

Discuss some rather off-the-wall remedies you have heard of. What makes them unconventional?

Think of some biblical examples where God provided healing in rather unusual ways. For instance, see **2 Kings 5; 13:21; John 9:6–7;** and **Mark 8:23–25**. What was the overall message sent by each of these miracles concerning the kind of "medicine" used by God?

Grumble, Grumble, Grumble

From the last lesson, where we studied the staff of Moses, we have skipped forward almost 40 years. What led to this 40 years of wandering in the wilderness (**Numbers 13–14**)? What is the historical context of **Numbers 21**, that is, how close are they to the end of the 40 years? How should this have affected their outlook?

What happened to the Israelites in **Numbers 21:1–3**? What impact would this have had on national morale? How might it also have led to problems such as pride?

In **Numbers 21:4**, the people are going "around the land of Edom." Why? See **Numbers 20:14–21**. What is the relationship between Israel and the Edomites? Think back to their "founders," Jacob and Esau.

Look in a Bible atlas to trace the roundabout route the Israelites were forced to take. What kind of impact did this have on the nation (**Numbers 21:4–5**)?

Look at verse 5 carefully. Against whom do the Israelites complain? The Hebrew word for *you* in "why have *you* brought us up" is plural. Compare this with the similar complaint of their fathers' generation in **Exodus 17:3** (where the you is singular). Which is the stronger complaint? What kind of twisted image of God do they describe? What indication does this give about how much the children are walking in the footsteps of their fathers?

What two contradictory things do the Israelites say about food in **Numbers 21:5**? What is the real problem with regard to food?

How is the incident described in **John 6:1–15** and **22–51** like this one in the wilderness? Look especially at **verses 41–43**. About what were the Israelites grumbling?

Both in **Numbers** and **John**, what did the people not trust? How are we the same way? How do we treat the gifts of God in creation? How do we treat the gifts of God in the church? How do we show our lack of trust? Give examples.

Fiery Serpents

What did the Lord do in response to the people's complaints (**Numbers 21:6**)? What kind of snakes were these? Why were they called "fiery" serpents?

The Bible speaks of three kinds of death. Look up these verses and describe each kind of death; note also if such a death is universal or if it only befalls some people: (a) **Ephesians 2:1–3**; (b) **Genesis 5**; (c) **Revelation 2:11; 20:6, 14–15; 21:8**. What kind(s) of death did the Israelites experience in the desert?

Repentance and Intercession

Psalm 78 is a poem that recalls the exodus. It records not only God's loving deeds, but also the rebellious deeds of the Israelites. In **verses 32–34**, what does the author say finally brought the people to repentance? What is it about death that finally brings some people to the point of confession?

Read the confession of the Israelites (**Numbers 21:7**). Is it complete? Do they speak truthfully? In what way is confession saying "Amen" back to God?

Why do the Israelites go to Moses and ask him to intercede? Why did the Israelites not pray for themselves? See **Exodus 32:11–14**; **Numbers 11:1–3, 14:13–19**. How is Moses like Jesus in this respect (**Romans 8:34**)?

What exactly did the Israelites ask Moses to pray for? What did they want God to do? Did He give them their request or something better? Do we always pray for what we truly need? How does God answer prayers such as these?

The Bronze Serpent

Imagine what the Israelites must have thought when Moses made the bronze serpent. To what might we compare this? It would be like a gunshot victim being told to look at a ______. Like a cancer patient being told to look at a ________. Give other examples.

Recall **Genesis 3**. How would this story have affected the Israelites' view of the bronze serpent?

As bizarre as this cure was to human eyes, there was divine wisdom in this choice. Discuss the following questions:

The Lord not only sent the punishment, but He also provided the cure. What does this tell us about the justice and mercy of our God?

What was the bronze serpent a graphic reminder of?

What did the Israelites have to "do" to be healed? What does this tell us about how God provides salvation? Compare with **Romans 6:8–9**.

Why did God use a symbol that would have appeared foolish in the eyes of the world? Compare with **1 Corinthians 1:18–31**.

Read **John 3:1–17** (especially **v. 14**) in light of **Numbers 21**. Discuss the following questions:

Here Jesus compares Himself to a serpent. How could such a lowly animal accurately represent Jesus? See **Isaiah 52:13–53:12**.

Why would Jesus liken Himself to something that hearkens back to Satan in **Genesis 3**? Why does the Messiah embody Satan's work of evil in this world in order to atone for that evil (**2 Corinthians 5:21**)?

How are we in a similar situation to the Israelites, yes, in an even worse situation? To what are we to look? Some would say we are to look to the "cross," but how can we see the cross now? How is the cross made "visible" today?

The Israelites who looked to the bronze serpent were healed; what does Jesus say we who believe in Him receive?

Consider the following quotation from Martin Luther.
In this way the Lord shows us the proper method of interpreting Moses and all the prophets. *He teaches us that Moses points and refers to Christ in all his stories and illustrations.* His purpose is to show that Christ is the point at the center of a circle, with all eyes inside the circle focused on Him. Whoever turns his eyes on Him finds his proper place in the circle of which Christ is the center. *All the stories of Holy Writ, if viewed aright, point to Christ.* During the forty days between Christ's resurrection and His ascension He expounded many similar texts and related many such stories to His disciples in His conversations with them (**Luke 24:27**). He did the same thing when He appeared on Mt. Tabor with Moses and Elijah (**Matthew 17:3**). Thus He also relates the figure of the serpent to Himself here. Thereby He opens the treasure chest of Moses and shows them the nugget concealed there. *He shows that all the stories and illustrations of Moses point to Christ.* The precious treasure of looking solely at Christ was so near and dear to Moses that he wore it, so to speak, between his skin and his flesh. (*Luther's Works, American Edition,* volume 22, page 340)
After this lesson and other lessons in this study, in what ways can you now better appreciate and affirm what Luther says? How has this opened up the Scriptures for you?

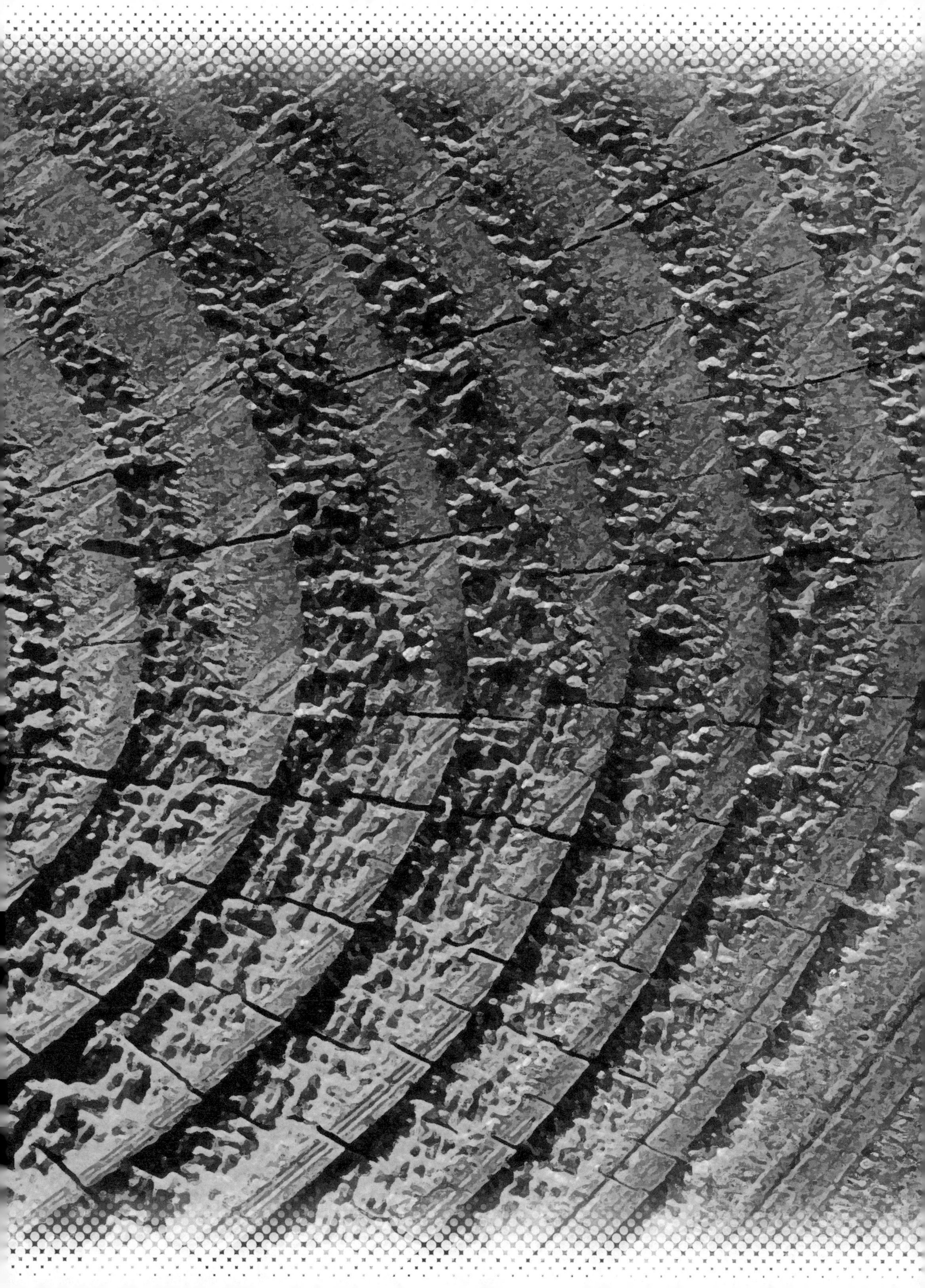

5

The Root and Shoot of Jesse

Prayer

Oh, come, O Rod of Jesse's stem,
From ev'ry foe deliver them
That trust Your mighty pow'r to save;
Bring them in vict'ry through the grave.
Rejoice! Rejoice! Emmanuel
Shall come to you, O Israel!

("Oh, Come, Oh, Come, Emmanuel," *LW* 31:4)

Family Trees

Discuss what a family tree is. Why do you think many people are so interested in their family history?

Years ago, my father became intensely interested in our family history. Though I was but a child at the time, his comments and stories about our forefathers led me to recognize even then what a fascinating study this could be. He collected pictures, wills, letters, and anything else he could obtain to shed light on who fit where in our family tree. What he found was a mixed bag. There was the occasional famous person who was in our family by blood or marriage, along with a multitude of others who quietly passed from this life into historical obscurity. Tracing the history backward was a most formidable, yet rewarding, task. If nothing else, such a history reminds one that no person is totally disconnected from others, any more than a twig can sprout in thin air. The twig is always attached to a branch, which is always attached to a larger branch, which is always attached eventually to the trunk, which is rooted in the soil. No man is a branch unto himself. He grows from the life of those who came before.

Talk about the place of the family in biblical history. What kinds of families are the focus? What is the purpose, for instance, of the many genealogies in the OT? Why do both Matthew (1:1–17) and Luke (3:23–38) include the genealogy of Jesus in their Gospels? Refamiliarize yourself with the 12 tribes of Israel. What is meant by the "12 tribes"? Who are they named after? Who is the father of all 12? Of these 12, which ones are the most familiar to you from biblical history?

In the Bible is planted a veritable forest of family trees. Already in the fourth chapter of the Scriptures we begin to hear about births. In the very next chapter, Genesis 5, the growing family tree of Adam and Eve is documented. So-and-so begat so-and-so who begat so-and-so. From father to son the sacred story goes onward, tracing the gradual growth of the human family. In Genesis 12, following another long list of births and deaths, the story narrows to one single branch on the ever-growing tree—the family of Abraham and Sarah. The rest of the Bible is chiefly concerned with this family. Abraham begat Isaac who begat Jacob who begat the 12 sons who became the 12 tribes of Israel. Though some stories focus more on one tribe or another, these dozen family groups are the primary concern of Genesis 12 through Malachi 4.

Along the way, however, one particular tribe gets special attention quite often—the tribe of Judah. Several biblical prophecies and stories highlight the centrality of this tribe in God's plan of salvation. For it is not only David who emerges from Judah as the ideal king over God's people, but also from this branch of Israel's tree that the new and better David, the Messiah, will spring forth.

Here we meet our next "tree" in biblical history—this time a different kind of tree, a family tree. But the tree is not merely a helpful metaphor chosen for the sake of simplicity; this is actually the language and imagery of the Bible itself. As we shall see in the prophet Isaiah, the Messiah is described both as the "root of Jesse [David's father]" (Isaiah 11:10) and the "shoot . . . from the stump of Jesse" (Isaiah 11:1). He emerges from this particular family to sprout upward, to grow into a tree, under which we all shall find divine shade and in whose branches there flourishes an abundance of saving fruit.

The Man Judah

Briefly scan the chapters that describe the birth of the sons of Jacob (Genesis 29–30). How many mothers are involved in bearing these children? Were they all the wives of one man? Why was bearing sons so important to Rachel and Leah? Who was the mother of Judah?

Though all from one father, Jacob's (a.k.a. Israel's) 12 sons came from not one, not two, not even three different mothers, but four: Rachel, Leah, Bilhah, and Zilpah. The first two mothers, Rachel and Leah, were sisters whom Jacob married while working for his father-in-law Laban (Genesis 29). There was a bitter competition between these two wives; the rivalry concerned who would bear the most sons for their co-husband Jacob. To increase their "score," therefore, they also gave their respective maidservants, Bilhah and Zilpah, to Jacob to act as surrogate mothers. Between the four of them Jacob's dozen were conceived and born. Son number four, Judah, came forth from Leah's womb.

Read the story of Joseph being sold by his brothers into slavery (Genesis 37:12–36). What role did Judah have in this story? What might his speech and actions tell you about his personality, his relationship with Joseph, his motivations, and his place in the family?

Judah grew into a man who was not exactly a striking example of piety. For instance, when most of Joseph's jealous brothers wanted to kill "this dreamer," as they called him (Genesis 37:19), it was Judah who stepped forward with compassion on his lips but dollar signs in his eyes: "'What profit is it if we kill our brother and conceal his blood? Come, let us sell him to the Ishmaelites, and let not our hand be upon him, for he is our brother, our own flesh'" (Genesis 37:26–27). Judah got his way and Joseph got the shaft, or more precisely, the chains.

Read Genesis 38. What does this episode in the life of Judah reveal about the man as a father, father-in-law, and public figure? Characterize Judah solely upon what you know from Genesis 37–38. What kind of hopes for "greatness" are held out for him in these chapters?

Later, there was a very ugly incident involving Judah and his daughter-in-law Tamar (Genesis 38), an incident that sounds like an ancient version of a soap opera. After Tamar married two of Judah's sons in succession, both of whom God killed for their transgressions, Judah refused to give her his third son even though the law demanded that he do so. Tamar waited and waited until eventually she grew tired of Judah's stalling. So with all the trickery she could muster, Tamar disguised herself as a prostitute, provided her services to unwitting Judah, and in the process became pregnant with her father-in-law's child. When he heard of Tamar's pregnancy out of wedlock, Judah put on quite a show of righteous indignation, but the cat was soon out of the bag. Tamar revealed whose DNA this child bore. Red-faced, Judah had to confess his paternity. To his credit, Judah at least admitted that Tamar was more righteous than he.

Review the history of Joseph in Egypt. What happened to him? To whom was he sold? How did he suffer? What finally happened that brought him up to a high position in Egypt? When the brothers of Joseph went down into Egypt to purchase grain during the famine, how did Joseph respond to them (Genesis 42)? How did the brothers react? How do their words reveal that they do have consciences, that they are burdened with the guilt of what they did years before to Joseph?

The next occasion at which Judah is mentioned again involves Joseph, although this time the tables are turned (Genesis 42). After Joseph was sold by his brothers, the cross he bore was intensely heavy for many years; finally, God relieved him of his burden and exalted him to Pharaoh's right hand. Through the wise planning of Jacob's son, Egypt and her people were saved from starvation during an extended famine. This famine affected not only Egypt, but also Canaan, where Jacob and his remaining sons were still living. In dire need of food, Jacob sent his sons to Egypt to purchase grain. When they appeared before "Egyptianized" Joseph, he recognized them, but they had no clue who he was. He appeared to deal very severely with them, even imprisoning one of their number, then demanding they return and bring back their youngest brother Benjamin.

When it is time for the brothers to go down to Egypt a second time, their father is very hesitant to send them. Why (Genesis 43:1–14)?

What finally convinces Jacob to let them go? What does this new episode tell you about Judah? How is this different from his previous speech and actions?

Read Genesis 44. How is Judah a central character in this part of the story? Contrast this with his earlier actions. How has he improved? In what way is he different from the remainder of his brothers? Skip forward to Genesis 46:28. What does this tell you about Judah's place in the family from Jacob's point of view?

Once the brothers returned to Canaan, there was a great reluctance to go back to Egypt for fear that some evil would befall Benjamin, who was held very dear in the heart of old Jacob. Finally, Judah assumed responsibility. He told his father,

> *Send the boy [Benjamin] with me, and we will arise and go, that we may live and not die, both we and you and also our little ones. I will be a pledge of his safety. From my hand you shall require him. If I do not bring him back to you and set him before you, then let me bear the blame forever. If we had not delayed, we would now have returned twice. (Genesis 43:8–10)*

For the first time recorded, Judah acts out of love, putting his own life and future on the line for the good of others.

As the story unfolds, the picture of Judah improves more. Joseph arranges to arrest Benjamin and take him captive while the other brothers are released. But Judah will not stand for this. He becomes a mediator, even offering himself as a substitute for his youngest brother. He begs Joseph—whom he still thinks is just an Egyptian official, and not his brother—to take him instead of Benjamin, to place him behind bars instead, but not to imprison Benjamin. He knows that if anything happens to Benjamin, their father will die of a broken heart (Genesis 44:18–34). At this point Joseph can no longer control himself; he reveals amidst a flood of tears that he is their long-lost brother (Genesis 45:1–3).

Of all the brothers, Judah alone emerges as the one willing to sacrifice himself so that those others might go free and be saved from grief. It is quite telling that it is Judah who leads the pack when Jacob and all his family make the journey down to Egypt to join Joseph (Genesis 46:28). We see a preview here of the leadership that is to come from this tribe; 400 years later, when the nation of Israel leaves Mount Sinai to travel back to the Promised Land, Judah again is at the head (Numbers 2:9; 10:14). Though not the firstborn among his brothers, he assumed that divinely ordained place of headship. The branch of Judah in Israel's family tree was growing larger and more prominent with every passing generation.

The Prophetic Promise to the Tribe

Read through Genesis 49. What is the purpose of Jacob's words to each of his sons? Is it the person or the tribe of which Jacob is speaking, or both? Jacob sees these matters as taking place "in the last days" (Genesis 49:1 KJV). These same words, or words very similar to them, also occur frequently in later prophecies by Isaiah, Jeremiah, and others. For instance, what does Isaiah say will happen in the last days (Isaiah 2:1–4)? Of what time period is he speaking (Hebrews 12:22–24)? What does Jeremiah say the Lord will do in the last days (Jeremiah 31:33–34)? When are these words fulfilled (Luke 22:20; Hebrews 8:8–9:28)?

The importance of the tribe of Judah was forever made clear when aged Jacob gathered his 12 sons around him to speak to each of them about what was to come "in the last days" (Genesis 49:1 KJV). The phrase "in the last days" (which not all English translations render literally) is highly significant. Those exact words, or words virtually identical to them, are used later in Israel's history by prophets such as Isaiah and Jeremiah to describe the days of the Messiah. For instance, Isaiah tells us that "*in the last days* . . . the mountain of the LORD's house shall be established in the top of the mountains, and shall be exalted above the hills; and all nations shall flow unto it" (Isaiah 2:2 KJV, emphasis added). This mountain is Mount Zion, which foreshadows the holy Christian church where Christ is present with His people (Hebrews 12:22–24). Jeremiah likewise prophesies that in the latter days the Lord will establish a new covenant (Jeremiah 31:33–34), a new covenant given on the night our Lord instituted the holy Supper (Luke 22:20). Long before Isaiah or Jeremiah, however, Jacob had already been given a glimpse into those "last days." When he blessed Judah, he foretold that the Anointed One would come forth from this tribe in the time of the Messiah.

In Genesis 49, the three older brothers of Judah are addressed first—Reuben, Simeon, and Levi (49:2–7). What kind of "blessing" do these brothers receive? Why? For the background of Jacob's words, see Genesis 35:22 and Genesis 34. Given Judah's own not-so-perfect personal history (just think of his dealings with young Joseph and Tamar!), what might he have been expecting to hear from his father?

As the father begins to speak, he addresses Reuben first, then Simeon and Levi (Genesis 49:2–7). These three older brothers do not exactly get the best of news from their dying father. Though we are told that Jacob blessed "each [son] with the blessing suitable to him" (Genesis 49:28), his words sound more like a curse than anything else. There are historical allusions in each of them to past misdeeds. Reuben, the firstborn, was stained by the guilt of having committed adultery with his father's concubine Bilhah (Genesis 35:22). Bilhah was the mother of Dan and Naphtali, two of Reuben's brothers. Characterized as "unstable as water" by Jacob, he is told that he "shall not have preeminence" (Genesis 49:4). Simeon and Levi, next in line, also reap what they have sown. Years earlier, these two brothers had exacted a heartless revenge upon all the male residents of Shechem, the city where their sister Dinah had been raped (Genesis 34). Not only was this overkill (quite literally), but it was also done when the men of the city were recovering from the circumcision which they had endured as a result of a solemn agreement with Jacob's sons (Genesis 34:13–24). Their father curses their anger and cruel wrath.

Read carefully Jacob's words of blessing to Judah (Genesis 49:8–12). How is the overall tone of these words remarkably different from what the patriarch said to the three older brothers?

Fourth in line, Judah may have been growing nervous as he listened to his father hearken back to Reuben's lust and the bloody violence of Simeon and Levi. For Judah had anything but a clean slate. Had he not been the very one to suggest that Joseph—Jacob's favorite son—be sold into slavery? Then there was that infamous fathering of his own daughter-in-law's child. Would Jacob refer to this? Would he too hear words that would haunt him and his tribe throughout their days?

No, this was not to be, for God had other plans for Judah—much better and much bigger plans. To this son the father said:

> *Judah, your brothers shall praise you; your hand shall be on the neck of your enemies; your father's sons shall bow down before you. Judah is a lion's cub; from the prey, my son, you have gone up. He stooped down; he crouched as a lion and as a lioness; who dares rouse him? The scepter shall not depart from Judah, nor the ruler's staff from between his feet, until tribute comes to him; and to him shall be the obedience of the peoples. Binding his foal to the vine and his donkey's colt to the choice vine, he has washed his garments in wine and his vesture in the blood of grapes. His eyes are darker than wine, and his teeth whiter than milk. (Genesis 49:8–12)*

The tone of this blessing is radically different from the two that precede it. Here are true words of blessing! What the Lord is promising Judah is nothing short of miraculous.

The "Judah" being addressed in these words is not only the individual Judah whose personal history we have been discussing thus far; it is also the messianic "Judah" who will come from this tribe. Bearing this in mind, look at this blessing verse by verse. What does verse 8 tell you about the place of Judah among his brothers? Compare this with Philippians 2:10–11.

The first thing we ought to take note of is exactly who is addressed. On the surface, it is Judah himself, the son of Jacob and Leah. But these words extend far beyond this sole individual. They are spoken *to him*, to be sure, but we might say more accurately that they are addressed *through him* to someone and about someone else. This "someone else," as we shall see, is the Messiah. He will have His earthly origin in Judah's tribe. He will sum up the whole tribe, indeed, the whole of Israel and humanity in Himself. Here He is named "Judah," as elsewhere in the Old Testament He is called "David" (Jeremiah 30:9; Ezekiel 34:24; 37:24; Hosea 3:5) and "Immanuel" (Isaiah 7:14). But this new, messianic Judah will succeed where His namesake failed. In Him all Israel will be blessed.

Jacob's blessing sounds the keynote up front: "Judah, your brothers shall praise you; your hand shall be on the neck of your enemies; your father's sons shall bow down before you." Judah will leave no foe unconquered, even as our Lord overwhelmed and destroyed the power of the devil, the might of sin, and the tyranny of death. All these He vanquished in His death and resurrection. In the face of this triumph, those around Him will offer up the sacrifice of praise. Every knee shall bow, and every tongue confess to the glory of God the Father that this messianic Judah, Jesus Christ, is Yahweh, the Lord Himself (Philippians 2:10–11).

How is Judah pictured in verse 9? What kinds of characteristics do you associate with this animal? Read this verse in light of Christ's passion. How does this Lion conquer His prey and defeat His enemies? For an insight, compare this verse with Revelation 5:1–10. By means of which two animals is Christ described? How is Jesus both? How do each of them depict the work of the Messiah?

Jacob proceeds to picture Judah as a regal lion. He shall overcome His prey as easily as this king of beasts. But how wondrously mysterious is the victory of the messianic Judah! For it is a victory gained in apparent defeat. This lion conquers by suffering death. He allows the wolves of hell to empty His veins. He lets the beasts of Satan trample Him underfoot. But in all this He is wise, like the wise Lion, Aslan, in C. S. Lewis's *The Chronicles of Narnia*. For it is in death that life comes forth, and it is in defeat that victory ensues. For this kingly Lion is also a sacrificial Lamb. Notice how St. John blends both pictures together in the following scene from Revelation 5:

> *Then I saw in the right hand of Him who was seated on the throne a scroll written within and on the back, sealed with seven seals. And I saw a strong angel proclaiming with a loud voice, "Who is worthy to open the scroll and break its seals?" And no one in heaven or on earth or under the earth was able to open the scroll or to look into it, and I began to weep loudly because no one was found worthy to open the scroll or to look into it. And one of the elders said to me, "Weep no more; behold, the Lion of the tribe of Judah, the Root of David, has conquered, so that He can open the scroll and its seven seals."*
>
> *And between the throne and the four living creatures and among the elders I saw a Lamb standing, as though it had been slain, with seven horns and with seven eyes, which are the seven spirits of God sent out into all the earth. And He went and took the scroll from the right hand of Him who was seated on the throne. And when He had taken the scroll, the four living creatures and the twenty-four elders fell down before the Lamb, each holding a harp, and golden bowls full of incense, which are the prayers of the saints. And they sang a new song, saying, "Worthy are You to take the scroll and to open its seals, for You were slain, and by Your blood You ransomed people for God from every tribe and language and people and nation, and You have made them a kingdom and priests to our God, and they shall reign on the earth." (Revelation 5:1–10)*

He is the "Lion of the tribe of Judah" (Revelation 5:5) while simultaneously the "Lamb standing, as though it had been slain" (Revelation 5:6). This Lion-Lamb is the messianic Judah of whom Jacob speaks.

How does Genesis 49:10 expand on 49:8? Who bows down to Judah here? What does this tell you about the reign of the Messiah? What characterizes His kingdom? How is it different from the kingdoms of this world?

What kinds of images are employed in verses 11–12? What does this suggest about the kingdom of the Messiah? What does each of the images have to say about the richness of the kingdom? How does this picture suggest an Eden-like setting?

In the words that follow, the rule of Judah is assured. Not only his brothers shall bow down before him (Genesis 49:8); the peoples shall be obedient to his word (Genesis 49:10). But the rule of the messianic Judah is not of this world, nor like the kingdoms of this age. For He rules not by tyranny, but by His Word of grace and life. His kingdom is not for the high and mighty, but the meek, the lowly, the sinner. This Friend and King of sinners welcomes all to His throne of grace, yes, even His table, where He feeds them with the choicest of meats and the finest of wines, the food of His body and the wine of His blood.

As Jacob finalizes the blessing, he paints a picture of paradise surrounding this new and better Judah. So Eden-like is the kingdom of this messianic Judah that vineyards fill the land. He ties His donkey's colt to the choice vine, unafraid of injuring it. He washes His garments in the blood of grapes. His eyes are darker than wine, his teeth whiter than milk. This poetic portrayal of the richness of the Messiah's kingdom exceeds all human imagining. Yet it has come at an equally unimaginable price. His kingdom is rich with wine for He Himself endured the agony of thirst on the cross. His garments are washed in wine for first He was stripped of all garments and washed in His own blood. His eyes are darker than wine but they first grew dark in death. And the teeth whiter than milk were stained with the blood from His bleeding face, split open by the fists of ungodly men. Eden was restored, but only after this Judah endured Eden's fiery opposite on the cross of wrath.

All these things—and more—are what Jacob prophesied of the Judah-to-come. The tribe of Jacob's son was divinely ordained to be the tribe of God's Son. It was only a matter of time before this messianic twig sprouted from the branch.

The Branch Narrows

Here we skip forward several generations. After the exodus, the partial conquest of Canaan, and the period of the judges, the people of Israel demanded that God give them a king so that they could be like the nations (1 Samuel 8:5). After having warned them of the consequences of such a ruler (1 Samuel 8:11–18), God gave them what they requested: Saul was anointed as the first king of Israel. As the Book of 1 Samuel makes painfully clear, this man failed to live up to what a king should be. He would be replaced by David. Review the early life of this son of Jesse. What made him famous? What did he accomplish in the first few years of his reign?

Down into Egypt went Judah, along with all his brothers and their father. There the people of Israel grew by leaps and bounds. Then came the oppression, the call of Moses, the plagues, the exodus, the 40-year pilgrimage, and then finally the entrance into the Promised Land. Under Joshua's leadership, the 12 tribes began a gradual conquest of the pagan peoples whose vile practices had polluted the land. A complete conquest, however, never was realized. After the death of Joshua, several areas were still under the control of the native population. Once again, the tribe of Judah took the lead in conquering and expelling the nations within the borders of Canaan (Judges 1). Their leadership, however, still did not bear the fruit of a total conquest.

Over time, warfare gave way to an ungodly peace. This peace was ungodly because God had not commanded it. He had commanded a complete expulsion, but the Israelites began to marry Canaanites, Hittites, Hivites, and all the other pagan "-ites" that lived in the land. Then came the period of the judges, in which a continuous cycle of *R*'s dominated Israel's history: Rebellion of Israel; Retribution by God; Repentance of Israel; Rescue by God; Rest for a period of years. At the end of this period the people requested a king so that they could be just like the other nations around them (1 Samuel 8:5). God conceded to their request, warning them through the prophet Samuel that a king would only make things worse. And so it was, for the king they received was Saul. Although he received high marks during the opening years of his reign, after several instances of outright rebellion against the Word of God Samuel announced that the kingdom would be ripped away from Saul and given to another man. That man was David.

With David the biblical story returns to the family tree of Judah. David was from that tribe, a son of Jesse, born in Bethlehem. The youngest son in a household of eight sons, David was not the logical choice for king. But the Lord does not make decisions based on logic but rather on divine wisdom, a wisdom that is foolishness to the world.

Though David's rise to kingship is fascinating in and of itself, it is his lineage and a divine promise extended to him that will be the focus of our attention for now. After Saul had fallen on the battlefield, his son assumed the throne, but not for long. In a few short years David was the sole king of Israel. He vanquished enemy after enemy, expanded the borders of Israel, and moved the capital to Jerusalem, a city formerly belonging to the Jebusites. Everything seemed to be going in his favor. It was then that he decided to construct a temple, a house for the Lord. Up to this time, the tabernacle had served as the meeting place between God and man. Though but a tent, the Lord had chosen it as the dwelling place of His presence.

Read 2 Samuel 7:1–17. How would you paraphrase the promises in verses 9–16? What does David want to do for the Lord? What does God instead promise to do for David? What kind of "house" will the Lord build for David? Whom will God use to build this house?

Compare the promise in 2 Samuel 7 with Luke 1:31–33. How are these words from the archangel linked to this promise to David? From which part of the promise to David is the author of Hebrews 1:5 quoting?

David approached the prophet Nathan with his desire and plan. He said, "See now, I dwell in a house of cedar, but the ark of God dwells in a tent." And Nathan said to the king, "Go, do all that is in your heart, for the LORD is with you" (2 Samuel 7:3). But hardly had Nathan given his own "okay" before God revealed to him a different plan:

> *That same night the word of the LORD came to Nathan, "Go and tell my servant David, 'Thus says the LORD: Would you build Me a house to dwell in? I have not lived in a house since the day I brought up the people of Israel from Egypt to this day, but I have been moving about in a tent for My dwelling. In all places where I have moved with all the people of Israel, did I speak a word with any of the judges of Israel, whom I commanded to shepherd My people Israel, saying, "Why have you not built Me a house of cedar?"' Now, therefore, thus you shall say to My servant David, 'Thus says the LORD of hosts, I took you from the pasture, from following the sheep, that you should be prince over My people Israel. And I have been with you wherever you went and have cut off all your enemies from before you. And I will make for you a great name, like the name of the great ones of the earth. And I will appoint a place for My people Israel and will plant them, so that they may dwell in their own place and be disturbed no more. And violent men shall afflict them no more, as formerly, from the time that I appointed judges over My people Israel. And I will give you rest from all your enemies. Moreover, the LORD declares to you that the LORD will make you a house. When your days are fulfilled and you lie down with your fathers, I will raise up your offspring after you, who shall come from your body, and I will establish his kingdom. He shall build a house for My name, and I will establish the throne of his kingdom forever. I will be to him a father, and he shall be to Me a son. When he commits iniquity, I will discipline him with the rod of men, with the stripes of the sons of men, but My steadfast love will not depart from him, as I took it from Saul, whom I put away from before you. And your house and your kingdom shall be made sure forever before Me. Your throne shall be established forever.'" In accordance with all these words, and in accordance with all this vision, Nathan spoke to David. (2 Samuel 7:4–17)*

We might paraphrase the Lord's words to David in this way:

> *You, O David, want to build Me a house of wood and stone. You, however, will not build Me a house; I myself will build you one, the "house"*

of a kingdom. I will raise up your son after you. He will build a house for My name and I will establish his kingdom. I will be his father and he will be My son.

How are the various promises to David fulfilled in the Messiah? What is the Messiah's "house" (Matthew 16:18)? How is He the son of David but also the Son of God (Romans 1:1–4)? How was He disciplined with the rods and stripes of men not for His own iniquity but for that which He took upon Himself (2 Corinthians 5:21; Isaiah 52:13–53:12)?

In a twofold way this prophecy points forward to what is to come. On the one hand, the *words of the prophecy* foretell the birth of the great Son of David and Son of the Father who will establish the kingdom of the church. As the archangel Gabriel tells the Virgin Mary: "And behold, you will conceive in your womb and bear a son, and you shall call His name Jesus. He will be great and will be called the Son of the Most High. And *the Lord God will give to Him the throne of His father David, and He will reign over the house of Jacob forever,* and of His kingdom there will be no end" (Luke 1:31–33, emphasis added). On the other hand, the prophecy is accompanied by *historical actions,* which also point forward to what is to come. These actions are the birth of another son of David, Solomon, who builds a house for the name of the Lord, that is, the temple (2 Chronicles 6:1–11). Together, the prophecy and the historical acts foretell and foreshadow the coming of the Messiah and the establishment of His kingdom.

Trace how the promise of the Messiah's "family tree" has gradually narrowed from the time of Adam and Eve to the time of David. What purpose did this narrowing serve? How did it help the people as they awaited the Messiah (see Matthew 2:1–6; Luke 2:1–5)?

What does this have to do with Judah's family tree? Everything! For up to this time, no one knew from which of the many families within the tribe of Judah the Christ would come. The possibilities were numerous. At the time of the exodus, there were already 74,600 people in Judah's tribe, from no telling how many different clans and families (Numbers 1:26–27). But the list of possibilities narrowed greatly with this promise to David. For now the Israelites knew that it would be from David's seed that the Messiah would come.

A Promise Made Is a Promise Kept

Though David was a good king, most of his heirs to the throne were not. What were these kings like? What led to their downfall? What temptations did they face and give into?

For about the next 400 years, many sons of David sat on the throne of his kingdom, but none of them was the Promised Seed. In fact, by and large the sons of David, as well as his grandsons, great-grandsons, and so forth, were miserable failures. Though each of them was intended to exemplify the pattern that the Messiah was to fulfill perfectly, they were not equal to the task. Solomon was led astray by his many pagan wives and his love of luxury. His arrogant son, Rehoboam, incited civil war in Israel, resulting in a split in the kingdom that was never healed. A downward spiral brought the nation closer and closer to the brink of disaster. At times, idols were worshiped even in the temple of Yahweh Himself. Pagan altars displaced the holy altar, the temple fell into disrepair, and even male and female cult prostitutes served up their own style of "worship" within the sacred precincts of the Lord's house. Forbidden alliances with neighboring nations were established for political gain. And that is only a sampling of the sad and sorry history recounted in 1 and 2 Kings. Although there were a couple of exemplary kings (Josiah and Hezekiah) and a handful of good-to-average kings, most deserved a big fat *F* on their regal report card. The limb of Judah, from which had sprouted the branch of David's family, looked more and more like a piece of deadwood fit only as fuel for the fire of God's wrath.

Given the woeful failures of the majority of the kings in David's line, the common Israelite may have begun to wonder if God would stick to His promise to keep the family tree of David

alive. How does Psalm 89 answer this question?

But Yahweh had made a promise to David that He planned to keep—indeed, that He had sworn to keep. These select verses from Psalm 89 make that abundantly clear:

> *I have found David, My servant; with My holy oil I have anointed him . . . My steadfast love I will keep for him forever, and My covenant will stand firm for him. I will establish his offspring forever and his throne as the days of the heavens. If his children forsake My law and do not walk according to My rules, if they violate My statutes and do not keep My commandments, then I will punish their transgression with the rod and their iniquity with stripes, but I will not remove from him My steadfast love or be false to My faithfulness. I will not violate My covenant or alter the word that went forth from My lips. Once for all I have sworn by My holiness; I will not lie to David. His offspring shall endure forever, his throne as long as the sun before Me. Like the moon it shall be established forever, a faithful witness in the skies. (Psalm 89:20, 28–37)*

Note well the resoluteness, the ironclad solidity of the Lord's promise: "My covenant will stand firm for him . . . I will not remove from him My steadfast love . . . I will not violate My covenant or alter the word that went forth from My lips . . . I will not lie to David." No waffling there! As it is impossible for God to lie, it was impossible for this promise from God to go unfulfilled. Even if David's offspring turned their backs on God, He would not turn His back on David. Even if David's family tree was cut down so that nothing remained but a seemingly lifeless stump, when the time came the green of life would emerge from that brown "dead" stump—the life of David's messianic Son.

The Root and Shoot of Jesse

Isaiah the prophet tells his readers in Isaiah 1:1 that he prophesied during the reigns of four kings: Uzziah, Jotham, Ahaz, and Hezekiah. These four heirs to the throne were all in the family tree of David. What did Uzziah do that made him infamous (2 Chronicles 26:16–23)? Why was his son Jotham not wholeheartedly commended (2 Chronicles 27:2)? What kind of king was Ahaz (2 Kings 16)? What good deeds did Hezekiah perform (2 Kings 18–20)? How would you characterize the overall picture of the kings during Isaiah's ministry? How might this have affected people's response to what Isaiah said about the promise to David?

It is the message of life from the dead that the prophet Isaiah announced in the eighth century B.C. This eloquent spokesman of God lived in the best of times and in the worst of times, as Charles Dickens might say. His ministry spanned in full or in part the reigns of four sons of David: Uzziah, Jotham, Ahaz, and Hezekiah (Isaiah 1:1). He saw the good, the bad, and the ugly from these kings. Uzziah (a.k.a. Azariah) managed fairly well until, drunk on his own power, he tried to usurp the priestly office by burning incense in the temple (2 Chronicles 26:16–23). The leprosy that broke out on his body as a result served as a painful reminder to the day of his death that one is not to snatch at what God has not given to him. Jotham his son was not a bad king, but neither was he at the top of his class. In his day "the people still followed [the] corrupt practices" (2 Chronicles 27:2) of their forefathers, such as frequenting the "high places" where the worship of Yahweh was mixed with the worship of other gods and goddesses (2 Kings 15:35). Of his son Ahaz, however, not a single good word is spoken. Indeed, the biblical historian uses plenty of ink to recount Ahaz's infamous deeds. Flagrant idolatry, bold-faced immorality, pandering to foreign rulers, child sacrifice—you name it, it's on Ahaz's rap sheet (2 Kings 16; 2 Chronicles 28). Thanks be to God, however, that the apple *did* fall far from the tree with his successor, Hezekiah. One of only two kings to receive an unconditional commendation, Hezekiah tried to fix everything his father had mangled and broken (2 Kings 18–20; 2 Chronicles 29–32). Unfortunately, however, when he was laid in his tomb, his rebellious son Manasseh followed in the footsteps of his grandfather Ahaz. Then Israel once more dove voluntarily into the sewer of religious and moral depravity.

During the reigns of each of these kings, there

lived close beside them in Jerusalem a man who saw through and beyond their time-bound reigns to the kingship of the One who would never leave the throne of David. Through the eye of the Spirit, he foresaw the coming downfall of the kingdom of Judah and of Judah's ruler, when the Assyrian and then the Babylonian axe would chop away at the tree of David, leaving only a stump sticking out of the earth. But more important, he also beheld a tiny green shoot emerge from the remains of this once great tree.

Read Isaiah 11:1–10. What do these verses say about the person and work of the Messiah? How do they characterize His reign, His judgment, and His gifts?

In one of his most well-known and best-loved chapters, Isaiah preaches about this coming "shoot"—who He is and what He will do:

> *There shall come forth a shoot from the stump of Jesse, and a branch from his roots shall bear fruit. And the Spirit of the LORD shall rest upon Him, the Spirit of wisdom and understanding, the Spirit of counsel and might, the Spirit of knowledge and the fear of the LORD. And His delight shall be in the fear of the LORD. He shall not judge by what His eyes see, or decide disputes by what His ears hear, but with righteousness He shall judge the poor, and decide with equity for the meek of the earth; and He shall strike the earth with the rod of His mouth, and with the breath of His lips He shall kill the wicked. Righteousness shall be the belt of His waist, and faithfulness the belt of His loins. The wolf shall dwell with the lamb, and the leopard shall lie down with the young goat, and the calf and the lion and the fattened calf together; and a little child shall lead them. The cow and the bear shall graze; their young shall lie down together; and the lion shall eat straw like the ox. The nursing child shall play over the hole of the cobra, and the weaned child shall put his hand on the adder's den. They shall not hurt or destroy . . . for the earth shall be full of the knowledge of the LORD as the waters cover the sea. In that day the root of Jesse, who shall stand as a signal for the peoples—of Him shall the nations inquire, and His resting place shall be glorious. (Isaiah 11:1–10)*

Here, in a beautiful, panoramic vision, the prophet places before our eyes the whole person and work of the Messiah. Filled with the sevenfold fullness of the Spirit of God, He will establish justice and righteousness in the earth. No enemy shall stand before Him, no liar deceive Him. A new and better Garden of Eden will reappear, created by Him and His work. To Him all peoples, Gentiles and Jews alike, will come to receive rest. All this we have in Christ and in His church. Though not yet fully revealed to the human eye, this reality is present and we participate in it. Before the Last Day, we live within the "now and the not yet"—the "now" of grace and blessing received by faith in the present and the "not yet" of our complete bliss in the future.

Look again at Isaiah 11:1. The Messiah is called a "shoot from the stump of Jesse." What does the image of a stump imply about the Davidic line? In what kind of shape would it be when the Messiah came? How does later history confirm this? Although he was not a descendant of David, King Herod was ruler over Israel when Jesus was born. What kind of ruler was he (Matthew 2:1–18)? Later in his book, Isaiah again describes the Messiah (53:2). In what way does this reaffirm what was said in 11:1?

In Isaiah 11:1, the Messiah is also called a "branch from his roots" that "shall bear fruit." What kind of fruit does the Messiah bear?

After a few more verses, Isaiah calls the Anointed One the "root of Jesse" (Isaiah 11:10). Compare this image with the one in 11:1. How can the Messiah be both the "root of Jesse" and the "shoot from the stump of Jesse"? How can He be both the source (root) of Jesse's life and also be born into Jesse's family? See Romans 1:1–4.

How is the Messiah a "signal for the peoples" (Isaiah 11:10)? Note that the Hebrew word used here for "signal" is the same word used to describe the "pole" upon which the bronze serpent was placed (Numbers 21:8). How are

these two signal poles similar? What is found under the shade of this Jesus-tree?

Compare the verses from Isaiah with Revelation 5:5 and 22:16. In what way do these verses confirm and add to what Isaiah preached?

Within these deep, rich verses, direct your attention especially to the beginning and the end. "There shall come forth a shoot from the stump of Jesse, and a branch from his roots shall bear fruit . . . In that day the root of Jesse, who shall stand as a signal for the peoples—of Him shall the nations inquire, and His resting place shall be glorious" (Isaiah 11:1,10).

Isaiah prophesies the coming of a "shoot from the stump of Jesse." He sees that time, mentioned above, when the axe of enemy nations would chop down the family tree of David. Only the stump of the tree would remain. Luther comments that Isaiah "points to a time in which the spiritual kingdom is to have its beginning, namely, when the stump of David will be regarded as lost, so that *nothing is less hoped* for than that a shoot should sprout up from the root" (AE 16:118, emphasis added). Thus, when Israel had had no Davidic son on the throne for over five hundred years; when a bloodthirsty, half-Jewish, more-than-half-crazed murderer named Herod was ruler over Israel; when a poor teenager from the backwoods of Judah was spending a cold night in a Bethlehem barn; when *nothing less would have been hoped for* than green growth from David's family stump; then "suddenly there was . . . a multitude of the heavenly host praising God, and saying, 'Glory to God in the highest, and on earth peace among those with whom He is pleased'" (Luke 2:13–14). The Son of David was born! A Shoot sprang forth from the stump of Jesse! As Isaiah wrote: "For He grew up before Him like a young plant, and like a root out of dry ground; He had no form or majesty that we should look at Him, and no beauty that we should desire Him" (Isaiah 53:2).

This baby boy was without form or majesty or beauty, yet hidden in Him were all the promises of the Father, made ages ago, which had finally come to pass. He had come to "bear fruit"—to bear fruit as a new and better Tree of Life. For the fruit of this Davidic Tree is forgiveness of sins, everlasting life, salvation, peace, and reconciliation with the Father.

But there is still more, for this "shoot from the stump of Jesse" is *at the same time* "the root of Jesse." But how can that be? How can He be both the shoot and the root, the source and the offspring? There is only one way: He must be both divine and human, God and man in one person. He is the Root of Jesse: the Creator, the source of this man's tribe and family, the One in whom Jesse and David lived and moved and had their being. But He is also the Shoot of Jesse: the One incarnate by the Holy Spirit of the Virgin Mary, who, as St. Paul says, "was descended from David according to the flesh" (Romans 1:3). To use the language of the Athanasian Creed, He is "God of the substance of the Father, begotten before the worlds; and man of the substance of His mother, born in the world; perfect God and perfect man . . . ." (*LW*, p. 135).

This God-man stands as a signal for the peoples. The Hebrew word translated here as "signal" is the same word we saw in the earlier lesson on the bronze serpent; there it was translated as "pole," the wooden signal upon which the serpent was to be mounted (Numbers 21:8). As that pole upheld the serpent as the medium of divine healing for Israel, so the "Root of Jesse" will provide a healing of His own. It will be healing from the toil of Adam's curse, the pain that plagues the world on account of sin, for "His resting place shall be glorious." And this healing will be not only for Israel, but also for "the nations," that is, for the Gentiles who seek Him.

And what will they find when they seek Him? What He Himself promises: "Come unto Me, all ye that labor and are heavy laden, and I will give you rest" (Matthew 11:28 KJV). There is rest beneath the boughs of this Jesus-tree. For Christ "is your keeper; the LORD is your shade on your right hand. The sun shall not strike you by day, nor the moon by night" (Psalm 121:5–6). In His branches and under His leaves there is nothing but peace, life, and wholeness.

We would do well to conclude this section with two verses from Revelation that echo the words of Isaiah:

> And one of the elders said to me, "Weep no more; behold, the Lion of the tribe of Judah, the Root of David, has conquered, so that He can open the scroll and its seven seals." (Revelation 5:5)
>
> "I, Jesus, have sent My angel to testify to you about these things for the churches. I am the root and the descendant of David, the bright morning star." (Revelation 22:16)

There He stands, with His own lips identifying Himself as the "Root of David" and the "root and the descendant of David." Sitting upon the throne of the kingdom, first the throne of the cross and now the throne of the Father, He rules over us in grace and mercy. The promise to Judah, the oath to David, has been fulfilled. The tree of Christ stands forever.

Conclusion

In the biblical history of family trees, it is the tree of Christ that makes all the difference. As the story progresses from the promise of a Seed to Adam and Eve to the promise of a direct descendant of David, we see God at work preparing His people for the arrival of the Messiah. Though when He arrives He is hidden in obscurity, a tiny green twig on the dead stump of Jesse, who and what He is becomes clear as He grows. He is the Anointed One, David's Son yet David's Lord, the One in whom sinners find rest and peace and the Kingdom without end.

Prayer

O Root of Jesse, standing as an ensign before the peoples, before whom all kings are mute, to whom the nations will do homage: Come quickly to deliver us. [Amen.]

(Psalm Antiphon for December 19, *LW*, p. 289)

The Root and Shoot of Jesse

Family Trees

Discuss what a family tree is. Why do you think many people are so interested in their family history?

Talk about the place of the family in biblical history. What kinds of families are the focus? What is the purpose, for instance, of the many genealogies in the OT? Why do both **Matthew (1:1–17)** and **Luke (3:23–38)** include the genealogy of Jesus in their Gospels?

Refamiliarize yourself with the twelve tribes of Israel. What is meant by the "12 tribes"? Who are they named after? Who is the father of all 12? Of these 12, which ones are the most familiar to you from biblical history?

The Man Judah

Briefly scan the chapters that describe the birth of the sons of Jacob (**Genesis 29–30**). How many mothers are involved in bearing these children? Were they all the wives of one man? Why was bearing sons so important to Rachel and Leah? Who was the mother of Judah?

Read the story of Joseph being sold by his brothers into slavery (**Genesis 37:12–36**). What role did Judah have in this story? What might his speech and actions tell you about his personality, relationship with Joseph, his motivations, and his place in the family?

Read **Genesis 38**. What does this episode in the life of Judah reveal about the man as a father, father-in-law, and public figure? Characterize Judah solely upon what you know from **Genesis 37–38**. What kind of hopes for "greatness" are held out for him in these chapters?

Review the history of Joseph in Egypt. What happened to him? To whom was he sold? How did he suffer? What finally happened that brought him up to a high position in Egypt?

When the brothers of Joseph went down into Egypt to purchase grain during the famine, how did Joseph respond to them (**Genesis 42**)? How did the brothers react? How do their words reveal that they do have consciences, that they are burdened with the guilt of what they did years before to Joseph?

When it is time for the brothers to go down to Egypt a second time, their father is very hesitant to send them. Why (**Genesis 43:1–14**)? What finally convinces Jacob to let them go? What does this new episode tell you about Judah? How is this different from his previous speech and actions?

Read **Genesis 44**. How is Judah a central character in this part of the story? Contrast this with his earlier actions. How has he improved? In what way is he different from the remainder of his brothers? Skip forward to **Genesis 46:28**. What does this tell you about Judah's place in the family from Jacob's point of view?

The Prophetic Promise to the Tribe

Read through **Genesis 49**. What is the purpose of Jacob's words to each of his sons? Is it the person or the tribe of which Jacob is speaking, or both? Jacob sees these matters as taking place "in the last days" (**Genesis 49:1 KJV**). These same words, or words very similar to them, also occur frequently in later prophecies by Isaiah, Jeremiah, and others. For instance, what does Isaiah say will happen in the last days (**Isaiah 2:1–4**)? Of what time period is he speaking (**Hebrews 12:22–24**)? What does Jeremiah say the Lord will do in the last days (**Jeremiah 31:33–34**)? When are these words fulfilled (**Luke 22:20; Hebrews 8:8–9:28**)?

In **Genesis 49**, the three older brothers of Judah are addressed first: Reuben, Simeon, and Levi (**49:2–7**). What kind of "blessing" do these brothers receive? Why? For the background of Jacob's words, see **Genesis 35:22** and **Genesis 34**. Given Judah's own not-so-perfect personal history (just think of his dealings with young Joseph and Tamar!), what might he have been expecting to hear from his father?

Read carefully Jacob's words of blessing to Judah (**Genesis 49:8–12**). How is the overall tone of these words remarkably different from what the patriarch said to the three older brothers?

The "Judah" being addressed in these words is not only the individual Judah whose personal history we have been discussing thus far; it is also the messianic "Judah" who will come from this tribe. Bearing this in mind, look at this blessing verse by verse. What does verse 8 tell you about the place of Judah among his brothers? Compare this with **Philippians 2:10–11**.

How is Judah pictured in **verse 9**? What kinds of characteristics do you associate with this animal? Read this verse in light of Christ's passion. How does this Lion conquer His prey and defeat His enemies? For an insight, compare this verse with **Revelation 5:1–10**. By means of which two animals is Christ described? How is Jesus both? How do each of them depict the work of the Messiah?

How does **Genesis 49:10** expand on **49:8**? Who bows down to Judah here? What does this tell you about the reign of the Messiah? What characterizes His kingdom? How is it different from the kingdoms of this world?

What kinds of images are employed in **verses 11–12**? What does this suggest about the kingdom of the Messiah? What do each of the images have to say about the richness of the kingdom? How does this picture suggests an Eden-like setting?

The Branch Narrows

Here we skip forward several generations. After the exodus, the partial conquest of Canaan, and the period of the judges, the people of Israel demanded that God give them a king so that they could be like the nations (**1 Samuel 8:5**). After having warned them of the consequences of such a ruler (**1 Samuel 8:11–18**), God gave them what they requested: Saul was anointed as the first king of Israel. As the Book of 1 Samuel makes painfully clear, this man failed to live up to what a king should be. He would be replaced by David. Review the early life of this son of Jesse. What made him famous? What did he accomplish in the first few years of his reign?

Read **2 Samuel 7:1–17**. How would you paraphrase the promises in **verses 9–16**? What does David want to do for the Lord? What does God instead promise to do for David? What kind of "house" will the Lord build for David? Whom will God use to build this house?

Compare the promise in **2 Samuel 7** with **Luke 1:31–33**. How are these words from the archangel linked to this promise to David? From which part of the promise to David is the author of **Hebrews 1:5** quoting?

How are the various promises to David fulfilled in the Messiah? What is the Messiah's "house" (**Matthew 16:18**)? How is He the son of David but also the Son of God (**Romans 1:1–4**)? How was He disciplined with the rods and stripes of men not for His own iniquity but for that which He took upon Himself (**2 Corinthians 5:21; Isaiah 52:13–53:12**)?

Trace how the promise of the Messiah's "family tree" has gradually narrowed from the time of Adam and Eve to the time of David. What purpose did this narrowing serve? How did it help the people as they awaited the Messiah (see **Matthew 2:1–6**)?

A Promise Made Is a Promise Kept

Though David was a good king, most of his heirs to the throne were not. What were these kings like? What led to their downfall? What temptations did they face and give into?

Given the woeful failures of the majority of the kings in David's line, the common Israelite may have begun to wonder if God would stick to His promise to keep the family tree of David alive. How does **Psalm 89** answer this question?

The Root and Shoot of Jesse

Isaiah the prophet tells his readers in **Isaiah 1:1** that he prophesied during the reigns of four kings: Uzziah, Jotham, Ahaz, and Hezekiah. These four heirs to the throne were all in the family tree of David. What did Uzziah do that made him infamous (**2 Chronicles 26:16–23**)? Why was his son Jotham not wholeheartedly commended (**2 Chronicles 27:2**)? What kind of king was Ahaz (**2 Kings 16**)? What good deeds did Hezekiah perform (**2 Kings 18–20**)? How would you characterize the overall picture of the kings during Isaiah's ministry? How might this have affected people's response to what Isaiah said about the promise to David?

Read **Isaiah 11:1–10**. What do these verses say about the person and work of the Messiah? How do they characterize His reign, His judgment, and His gifts?

Look again at **Isaiah 11:1**. The Messiah is called a "shoot from the stump of Jesse." What does the image of a stump imply about the Davidic line? In what kind of shape would it be when the Messiah came? How does later history confirm this? Although he was not a descendant of David, King Herod was ruler over Israel when Jesus was born. What kind of ruler was he (**Matthew 2:1–18**)? Later in his book, Isaiah again describes the Messiah (**Isaiah 53:2**). In what way does this reaffirm what was said in **Isaiah 11:1**?

In **Isaiah 11:1**, the Messiah is also called a "branch from his roots" that "shall bear fruit." What kind of fruit does the Messiah bear?

After a few more verses, Isaiah calls the Anointed One the "root of Jesse" (**Isaiah 11:10**). Compare this image with the one in **11:1**. How can the Messiah be both the "root of Jesse" and the "shoot from the stump of Jesse"? How can He be both the source (root) of Jesse's life and also be born into Jesse's family? See **Romans 1:1–4**.

How is the Messiah a "signal for the peoples" (**11:10**)? Note that the Hebrew word used here for "signal" is the same word used to describe the "pole" upon which the bronze serpent was placed (**Numbers 21:8**). How are these two signal poles similar? What is found under the shade of this Jesus-tree?

Compare these verses from Isaiah with **Revelation 5:5** and **22:16**. In what way do these verses confirm and add to what Isaiah preached?

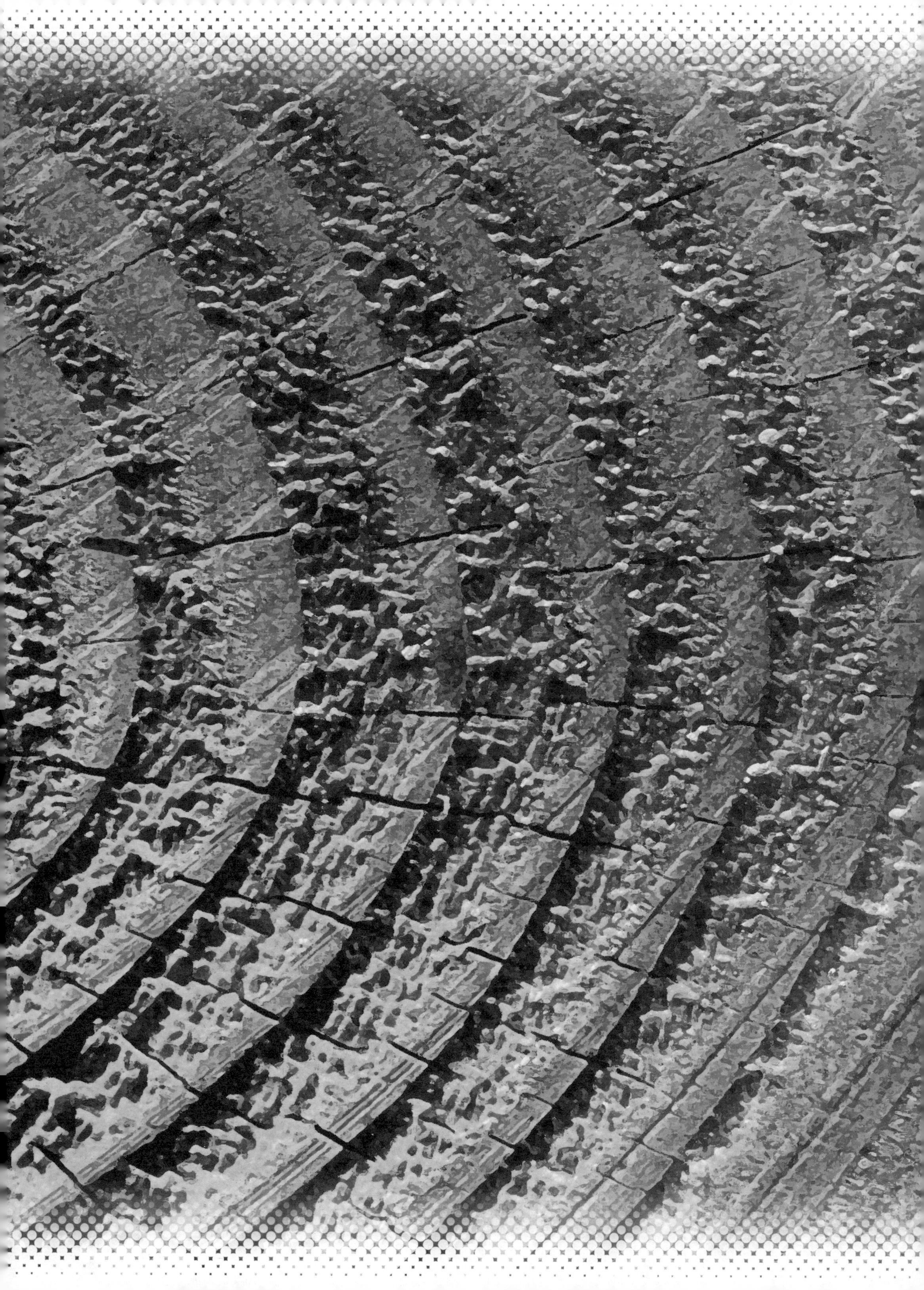

6

The Tree of the Cross

Prayer

Almighty and everlasting God, who hast willed that Thy Son should bear for us the pains of the cross that Thou mightest remove from us the power of the adversary, help us so to remember and give thanks for our Lord's Passion that we may obtain remission of sins and redemption from everlasting death; through the same Jesus Christ, Thy Son, our Lord, who liveth and reigneth with Thee and the Holy Ghost, ever one God, world without end. Amen.

(Collect for Good Friday, *TLH*, p. 67)

Born to Die

How would you summarize, in one or two sentences, the message of Christmas? Which hymns in the Christmas season convey this same message?

For most Christians, a Christmas without the singing of hymns and carols about the nativity of our Lord is simply inconceivable. From Martin Luther's "From Heaven Above to Earth I Come" (*TLH* 85; *LW* 37) to Isaac Watts's "Joy to the World" (*TLH* 87; *LW* 53), hymns of gladness and rejoicing echo throughout churches around the world. Common themes emerge even from a rapid glance at sacred songs such as these: the manger, the shepherds, Mary and Joseph, the town of Bethlehem, the angels, and, at the center of them all, the Son of God who came down from heaven to unite our flesh and blood to Himself. One Christmas hymn beautifully captures in four brief lines the great mystery of this Infant who is both fully divine and fully human:

> "Upon a manger filled with hay
> In poverty content He lay;
> With milk was fed the Lord of all,
> Who feeds the ravens when they call."
>
> ("Now Praise We Christ, the Holy One," *TLH* 104:5)

The church rightly lauds and magnifies the Father for this inexpressible gift!

Read aloud the stanzas from "What Child Is This" (*LW* 61). Compared to most other hymns about the nativity of our Lord, how is this hymn

different? What coming event does it speak of? Why is this an important point for a hymn to make?

While singing such hymns of joy and exultation, one often stumbles upon words that at first don't seem to fit. In fact, they jar the singer, almost shocking him into looking around to make sure the Christmas tree is still standing there, the church still decked out in white. A prime example of this is "What Child Is This" (*LW* 61). When we begin the hymn, our minds are led by the poetry to picture Mary, holding the sleeping infant Jesus in her lap. All is calm. Even the music bears the message of peace in its slow, sacred tones. Then, seemingly out of nowhere, we hear ourselves sing words that pulsate with the blows of hammers and violence:

"Nails, spear shall pierce Him through,
The cross be borne for me, for you;
Hail, hail the Word made flesh,
The babe, the son of Mary!"

("What Child Is This," *LW* 61:2)

Needless to say, nails and spears are not what most people think of when they gaze at a nativity scene! But they should. We all should. We must not let the serenity of the picture misguide us into forgetting the purpose for which this Infant came. For ultimately He did not come to be swaddled by His mother, but to be stripped by soldiers; He did not come to be gently kissed, but to be slapped and spat upon; He did not come to drink milk, but sour wine and the cup of His Father's wrath. That is why He descended from heaven—to suffer, die, and rise again, all for you. He came down for the nails, the spear, the thorns, the whips, the bleeding and the dying. He came with His eyes locked on the wood prepared for Him from the foundation of the world, the wood on which He would give up His life that we might be rescued from certain and everlasting death. It is the wood of this tree—the tree of the cross—that will be the focus of our attention in this final section. For it is that tree that towers above all other trees in Holy Scripture. On it our redemption is won.

The Friday Called "Good"

In the vast majority of churches, there are far more people in church on Easter than on Good Friday. Why is that? What is it that keeps people from church on Good Friday but brings them on Easter? What are the implications of this inequality?

It's a fact, sad but true, that Good Friday services are never as well-attended as those on Easter Sunday. If there is an exception somewhere out there, then thanks be to God. But I've yet to hear of it. There are multiple reasons for this inequality, of course, but ranking high on the list is this plain truth: people *do not like* the story of our Lord's crucifixion. Not, of course, that we should or must necessarily "like" it. How we "feel" or what we "like," however, are beside the point. The point is that people shun it. They hide their faces from it. It is more to their *liking*—there's that word again—to wait for the brightness of Easter morn, for the Alleluias to sound again, to hear the message of "He is risen" without ever really contemplating the question, "Risen *from what*?" So what really is "good" about "Good Friday"?

What is "good" about Good Friday? How would the world view this day? How does God view this day? As Jesus saw His cross approaching, how did He view it (Hebrews 12:2)? Can we rightly say that God was pleased to put His Son to death (Isaiah 53:10)? How can we say this?

The simple answer is that *everything is good* about Good Friday. It is good not if viewed *from below*, from the perspective of the world, but *from above*, from the viewpoint of heaven. For from below it must certainly be called "Bad Friday," the "Worst Friday Ever." For what can be good, asks a world of sinners, about mockery, shame, public nakedness, whips, nails, and thorns? What can be good about blood, blood, lots of blood, dripping from the grotesquely tortured body of Jesus? None of it can be good—unless it was done because of the goodness of God. And there is the key that unlocks the mystery of Good Friday's goodness. The author of Hebrews tells us that Jesus, "for the joy that was set before Him endured the cross, despising the shame, and is seated at the right hand of the throne of God" (Hebrews 12:2). What is this "joy" that was set before our Lord? Is it not the joy of your salvation, the joy of dying for the one whom He loves, the joy of giving up everything that you might have it all? That was the joy set before Him—you and your home in heaven with Him. All He did, all He suffered, was prompted by His goodness. For He "*is* good," as the psalmist can't repeat often enough.

That is the prism through which we must view the passion of our Lord. Should we weep at His death? There is nothing wrong with tears at such a time. Should we lament our sins that put Him there? Again, there is nothing wrong with repentance as we see His death unfold. But as we weep or lament, chant or sing, pray or quietly contemplate what He did, we must know and confess that it is *Good* Friday, for He is good and His steadfast love endures forever. In the end, we must voice our "Amen" to what the Father's good pleasure was, for as Isaiah says, "It pleased the Lord to bruise Him" (Isaiah 53:10 KJV). It pleased the Father for the same reason it pleased the Son and the Holy Spirit, for nothing pleases the Holy Trinity more than saving you.

On the Way to the Tree

There are many ways in which one could study the passion of Jesus. Ever since He bowed His head and gave up His spirit, I'm certain that not a single day has passed in which someone has not thought, prayed, written, sung, or preached about His death. That, in and of itself, is astounding. It is also humbling, for one can barely begin to explore the depths of His dying day in a few meager pages. But we shall make that beginning at least, focusing our attention on what we have been surveying all along: the place of wood and trees in His story.

Read Matthew 26:36–46. What has already transpired on this night? Where are Jesus and the disciples now?

We begin after our Lord celebrated the Passover with His disciples. According to their established custom, they went out to the Mount of Olives (Luke 22:39). Rising about 100 feet above the city on the eastern side, this "mountain" was more like a large hill. As the name suggests, the hillside was covered with olive trees. Among these trees was an area called Gethsemane (Matthew 26:36), which means "oil press," so named because the machinery by which oil was squeezed from the fruit was located here. In this garden, surrounded by trees, the intensity of our Lord's sufferings greatly increased. The evangelist Matthew depicts the scene:

> *Then Jesus went with them to a place called Gethsemane, and He said to His disciples, "Sit here, while I go over there and pray." And taking with Him Peter and the two sons of Zebedee, He began to be sorrowful and troubled. Then He said to them, "My soul is very sorrowful, even to death; remain here, and watch with Me." And going a little farther He fell on His face and prayed, saying, "My Father, if it be possible, let this cup pass from Me; nevertheless, not as I will, but as You will." And He came to the disciples and found them sleeping. And He said to Peter, "So, could you not watch with Me one hour? Watch and pray that you may not enter into temptation. The spirit indeed is willing, but the flesh is weak." Again, for the second time, He went away and prayed, "My Father, if this cannot pass unless I drink it, Your will be done." And again He came and found them sleeping, for their eyes were heavy. So, leaving them again, He went away and prayed for the third time, saying the same words again. Then He came to the disciples and said to them, "Sleep and take your rest later on. See, the hour is at hand, and the Son of Man is betrayed into the hands of sinners. Rise, let us be going; see, My betrayer is at hand." (Matthew 26:36–46)*

Hard and heavy was the burden pressing down upon our Lord. It was as if *He were the fruit* in the oil press that night, His body and soul compressed under the huge weight of our sins, squeezed until His blood began to seep from His pores. Indeed, the evangelist Luke says that "being in agony He prayed more earnestly; and His sweat became like great drops of blood falling down to the ground" (Luke 22:44). Yes, there in the garden His sufferings had begun in earnest.

What does Paul say about Adam and Christ in Romans 5:12–21? In what ways are they alike and in what ways are they different? Keeping in mind the corresponding relationship between the first Adam and the second Adam, how is it significant that Jesus began His most intense sufferings in a garden (cf. Genesis 2:8–3:24)?

In a garden, surrounded by trees, all human suffering had its genesis (Genesis 2:8–3:24). But now another Adam, a second and better Adam, had come down from heaven to undo what the first Adam had done so wrong. St. Paul says in his Letter to the Romans that Adam "was a *type* of the one who was to come" (5:14, emphasis added). As a type, he set a pattern that would in some way be followed by Christ. For instance, as Adam was a created "son of God" (Luke 3:38), so Christ is God's "beloved Son" (Luke 3:22); Adam was tempted by Satan (Genesis 3), as was our Lord Jesus (Luke 4:1–13); and as Adam's response to that temptation—sin—brought death, so Christ's response to temptation—obedience to His Father—brought universal life. St. Paul expresses it this way:

> *But the free gift is not like the trespass. For if many died through one man's trespass, much more have the grace of God and the free gift by the grace of that one man Jesus Christ abounded for many. And the free gift is not like the result of that one man's sin. For the judgment following one trespass brought condemnation, but the free gift following many trespasses brought justification. If, because of one man's trespass, death reigned through that one man, much more will those who receive the abundance of grace and the free gift of righteousness reign in life through the one man Jesus Christ. Therefore, as one trespass led to condemnation for all men, so one act of righteousness leads to justification and life for all men. For as by the one man's disobedience the many were made sinners, so by the one man's obedience the many will be made righteous. (Romans 5:15–19)*

For this reason, the church sings "In Him the tribes of Adam boast *More blessings* than their father lost" ("Jesus Shall Reign Where'er the Sun," *TLH* 511:5, emphasis added). Yes, "more blessings!" We gain more in the Second Adam than we lost in the first Adam, for He is both God and man, united in one person; in Him we have access to perfect righteousness and perfect peace that will never end. In Him we are actually made "partakers of the divine nature" (2 Peter 1:4)!

But it all came at a price, the dearest of prices. We were rescued from the devil "not with gold or silver, but with His holy, precious blood and with His innocent suffering and death," as Luther's Small Catechism teaches us to confess (Apostles' Creed, Explanation of the Second Article). Although His blood had been shed before this night (beginning already when He was eight days old, at His circumcision in Luke 2:21!), it would soon begin to pour from His body. And although He had suffered innocently before this (as when Herod tried to kill Him while He was yet an infant [Matthew 2:16–18]), now His suffering would increase in a way unfathomable to the human mind. In the end, the sins of Adam and Eve, and of all other "Adams" and "Eves," would be atoned for on the tree of the cross.

How fitting it was, therefore, for this Second Adam to begin His greatest suffering in a garden, surrounded by trees, where sin and suffering, death and misery, first raised their ugly heads in this once-perfect world. It was Genesis 3 all over again. Only this time, the story would have the happiest of endings.

Bearing the Wood

Read through the passion account of one of the four evangelists to see what happened after Jesus was arrested by the soldiers up until the moment He was led out to be crucified (Matthew 26:57–27:26; Mark 14:53–15:20; Luke 22:54–23:25; John 18:12–19:16).

Shortly after Jesus had prayed to His Father, a crowd of soldiers and ruffians stepped into the garden. Led by Jesus' own traitorous disciple, Judas Iscariot, they were there to arrest Him. This set in motion a number of events, each recorded by one or more of the four evangelists.

First, over-zealous Peter struck out with his sword in an attempt to protect his Master (John 18:10). His blade severed the ear of Malchus, a servant of the high priest. Malchus's ear was quickly reattached by our Lord, who struck back at *Peter's* ears with these sharp words: "Put your sword into its sheath; shall I not drink the cup that the Father has given Me to drink?" (John 18:11).

Bound by the soldiers, Jesus was led in the darkness from one "monkey court" to another. First He was taken to the home of Annas, father-in-law of the high priest, and then to Caiaphas, the high priest. There sham justice was administered, everything calculated to insure a guilty verdict. Each false witness, by his lies, greased the way for the next false witness. The whole mess was so contrived that even the testimony of these liars did not agree (Mark 14:56). This was no problem, however, for the leaders were thirsting for blood. Justice or no justice, they wanted Jesus dead. And they would have Him dead.

Early in the morning, after several dark hours of mockery, injustice, and physical violence, Jesus was led to Pilate, the Roman governor. Back and forth Pilate went with Jesus, and he was amazed at how little this "convict" was willing to cooperate in order to save His own neck. Though Pilate—quite the political animal—was initially willing to have Jesus beaten and then to release Him, the crowds gathered outside his headquarters would not stand for it. "Crucify, crucify Him!" they incessantly howled (Luke 23:21). Finally, caving in to the pressure, the Roman governor washed his hands of our Lord, delivering Him over to be crucified. So for ages now, the church has confessed in her creed that Jesus was "crucified under Pontius Pilate," an ever-present reminder of the infamy of a man who would bow before a bloodthirsty crowd rather than stand tall for justice.

Wearing the crown of thorns beaten into His head by the soldiers, the flesh of His back ripped to shreds by their iron-tipped whips, our Lord then began the walk to Golgotha, the place of execution. He went out, as St. John observes, "bearing His own cross" (John 19:17). Moving toward that place of sacrifice, Jesus was an innocent victim, "like a lamb that is led to the slaughter" (Isaiah 53:7). The Father would "not spare His own Son but [would give] Him up for us all" (Romans 8:32). Of the lineage of Abraham, this promised Son carried on His back the very wood that His lifeblood would soon stain crimson.

Now read Genesis 22:1–19 in light of the passion of our Lord. Note the parallels that exist between these two stories. What connections are there between fathers and sons? What geographical connection is there? Where was Mount Moriah, where Isaac was taken to be crucified? See 1 Chronicles 21:18–30; 2 Chronicles 3:1.

How are both Isaac and Jesus of the seed of Abraham? (See Genesis 12:7; 22:18; Galatians 3:16 KJV.) How were they both sons of promise? Compare Genesis 22:6 and John 19:17. What did both carry?

And as He did, this Son of Abraham followed a path already blazed centuries earlier by another promised son, another son of Abraham, who ascended his own mountain for the sacrifice commanded by God. As we read in Genesis 22:

After these things God tested Abraham and said to him, "Abraham!" And he said, "Here am I." He said, "Take your son, your only son Isaac, whom you love, and go to the land of Moriah, and offer him there as a burnt offering on one of the mountains of which I shall tell you." So Abraham rose early in the morning, saddled his donkey, and took two of his young men with him, and his son Isaac. And he cut the wood for the burnt offering and arose and went to the place of which God had told him. On the third day Abraham lifted up his eyes and saw the place from afar. Then Abraham said to his young men, "Stay here with the donkey; I and the boy will go over there and worship and come again to you." And Abraham took the wood of the burnt offering and laid it on Isaac his son. And he took in his hand the fire and the knife. So they went both of them together. And Isaac said to his father Abraham, "My father!" And he said, "Here am I, my son." He said, "Behold, the fire and the wood, but where is the lamb for a burnt offering?" Abraham said, "God will provide for Himself the lamb for a burnt offering, my son." So they went both of them together.

When they came to the place of which God had told him, Abraham built the altar there and laid the wood in order and bound Isaac his son and laid him on the altar, on top of the wood. Then Abraham reached out his hand and took the knife to slaughter his son. But the angel of the LORD called to him from heaven and said, "Abraham, Abraham!" And he said, "Here am I." He said, "Do not lay your hand on the boy or do anything to him, for now I know that you fear God, seeing you have not withheld your son, your only son, from Me." And Abraham lifted up his eyes and looked, and behold, behind him was a ram, caught in a thicket by his horns. And Abraham went and took the ram and offered it up as a burnt offering instead of his son. So Abraham called the name of that place, "The LORD will provide"; as it is said to this day, "On the mount of the LORD it shall be provided." (Genesis 22:1–14)

Read this story "backwards," from the future to the past, with the crucifixion of Jesus as the lens through which you see it. No doubt you will agree with Luther that here we see but a clear example of how "all the narratives of the Old Testament point so nicely and beautifully to Christ and confess Him" (AE 52:126). The *first* link between the stories of these two sons of Abraham is geographical, for Mount Moriah became the site of Jerusalem, the very city where Jesus was crucified! On this mountain David built an altar to avert divine wrath (1 Chronicles 21:18–30). Later his son Solomon built the temple, the sacrifices of which pointed forward to the sacrifice of Jesus (2 Chronicles 3:1). *Second,* both Isaac and Jesus were sons of promise; both are called the seed of Abraham (Genesis 12:7; 22:18; Galatians 3:16 KJV), and their births were long awaited and much anticipated. *Third,* as Isaac was Abraham's son, Abraham's only son, whom he loved, so Jesus is the Son, the only Son of His beloved heavenly Father. *Fourth,* contrary to every rational expectation, they are both led up to be sacrificed. *Lastly* (though we could keep going!), both carry their own wood for the sacrifice:

> And Abraham took the wood of the burnt offering and laid it on Isaac his son. (Genesis 22:6)
>
> So they took Jesus, and He went out, bearing His own cross. (John 19:16–17)

Yet how is the end of the story different for these two sons? In what way does the ram in Genesis 22 foreshadow Jesus? How are we like Isaac (Galatians 4:28)?

On Good Friday, desiring your salvation, your forgiveness, and your everlasting life with Him, *God* took the wood of the burnt offering and laid it on *Jesus* His Son. *Unlike* Isaac, of course, there was no "ram, caught in a thicket by his horns" to serve as a substitute for this other Son of Abraham. Rather, Jesus Himself was the Ram of God, caught by nails in the thicket of the cross. Caught? Yes, but willingly, for He preferred to die rather than spend eternity without all of you "Isaacs." For we are, as St. Paul tells us, "like Isaac . . . children of promise" (Galatians 4:28).

The Place of the Skull

Jesus was crucified at a place called "Golgotha" in Aramaic; this is translated "the place of the skull." Although rooted in tradition and not in the Bible, the older explanation of this name says that Golgotha was so named because it was *the place of Adam's skull,* that is, his grave. Remember what you read in Romans 5. Also read 1 Corinthians 15:22. Whether this tradition is true or not, how would the message it sends communicate the truth?

Our Lord was crucified between two thieves on a hill called, in Aramaic, Golgotha. Meaning "the place of the skull," Golgotha is typically identified today with a rocky outcropping near Jerusalem, the contours of which partially resemble a human skull. But this explanation is not the most ancient.

Although rooted in tradition and not in the Bible, the older explanation of this name says that Golgotha was so named because it was *the place of Adam's skull*, that is, his grave. Thus, according to this tradition, the Second Adam was crucified over the grave of the first Adam! Whether such a legend is true or not, no one knows. But what is *most certainly true* is the message that the story wishes to convey: that Jesus came as the new and better Adam to restore the life Adam had lost, to perfect it, and to make us participants in it. The tree by which Adam ended up in that grave was replaced by a new tree that brought Adam out of the grave, "for as in Adam all die, so also in Christ shall all be made alive" (1 Corinthians 15:22). On the tree of the cross Christ brought us back to *the knowledge of the good* once again: the good life, the good God, the good paradise that awaits us. Martin Luther speaks similarly as he relates the place of Christ's death to the Garden of Eden:

> *Thus the center of Paradise was where Jerusalem, Bethlehem, and Jericho were located later on, the places where Christ and John spent the greater part of their life . . . It is possible that later on Calvary, where Christ offered Himself for the sins of the world, was located where the tree of the knowledge of good and evil had been while Paradise was still standing. Thus so far as the place is concerned, death and destruction through Satan would be matched by life and salvation won through Christ. (AE 1:309)*

How might such a tradition also shed further light on Jesus' words to the repentant thief (Luke 23:43)?

With such a perspective, the words of Jesus to the penitent criminal being crucified alongside Him deepen in significance: "Assuredly, I say to you, today you will be with Me *in Paradise*" (Luke 23:43, emphasis added). Indeed, Paradise was regained that very day, on that very spot, for that man and for us all.

The Crucified Serpent

Although we studied earlier the account of Israel's rebellion in the wilderness, the divine punishment that came in the form of the fiery serpents, and the bronze serpent Moses attached to the uplifted pole, it is worth recalling at this point in our Lord's passion (Numbers 21:4–9).

Were you to have been watching that day, you would have seen the soldiers bring Jesus to the place of crucifixion. His hands (technically, His wrists) would have been nailed through. His feet too, punctured with iron spikes, would have been attached to the wood. It is likely that under His feet was a small piece of wood, sticking out from the cross as a sort of footrest. It was there, however, not out of sympathy, but only to postpone death and thus prolong suffering. He was riddled with wounds, as were many of those crucified by the Romans, for the soldiers were allowed to do what they wanted with the condemned. And "what they wanted" always led to blood. Above His head was the *titulus*, the sign on which Pilate had written, "Jesus of Nazareth, the King of the Jews" in Aramaic, Latin, and Greek (John 19:19–22). There He hung, hour after hour, speaking at least seven times—sometimes to His Father (Luke 23:34), sometimes to His own (John 19:26–27), sometimes to those who crucified and mocked Him (John 19:28). Finally, at the ninth hour (3:00 P.M.), after three hours of darkness, He said, "'It is finished,' and He bowed His head and gave up His spirit" (John 19:30).

That is what you would have seen with the naked eye. That is what those crowded around the place—friend, foe, and stranger—would have heard and seen. But there was more. Hidden from the *naked* human eye, visible only to the eye *clothed* by the Word of God, was a far deeper reality.

Now that that passion account is fresh in your mind, recall what you studied in Numbers 21 and John 3:14 with regard to the bronze serpent. In what way is Jesus our "Serpent of salvation," as Luther called Him?

You will recall the words Jesus spoke to Nicodemus on the night this member of the Sanhedrin came to see the One he called "Rabbi": "As Moses lifted up the serpent in the wilderness, so must the Son of Man be lifted up, that whoever believes in Him may have eternal life" (John 3:14–15). On that Good Friday a new Serpent was lifted up, the one Luther called our "Serpent of salvation" (AE 22:340). As Moses lifted up the serpent in the wilderness atop a pole in the midst of Israel's camp, so this Serpent was lifted up atop a cross in the midst of Israel. Whoever looked to that bronze serpent in faith lived, even as those who believe in our crucified Lord have eternal life. For there He truly became all the poison, all the death, all the sin, that was not His own, but ours. We who rightly deserve the title "brood of vipers" (Luke 3:7) have our snake-like nature transformed so that we become children of God, while the true Son of God trades places with us, becoming the viper on our behalf. God "made Him to be sin who knew no sin, so that in Him we might become the righteousness of God" (2 Corinthians 5:21). He becomes what we are that we might become what He is.

He Is Not Here

Read the account of our Lord's resurrection in one of the four Gospels. Why was it necessary for our Lord to be raised again (Acts 2:24–31)? How do we participate in both the crucifixion and the resurrection of Jesus (Romans 6:1–11)?

But thanks be to God that the story does not end there! The Garden of Eden re-created for us, the wood borne up the hill by the Second Isaac, Adam's evildoing undone at Golgotha. The Serpent, having been lifted up on the crucifixion pole, finished His work of atonement. Resting in the tomb for the remainder of Friday, the Sabbath, and part of the day on Sunday, He then arose victorious over all His foes. "He is not here, for He has risen," as the angel announced at the empty tomb (Matthew 28:6).

So complete is the defeat of Satan, so utterly vanquished are sin, death, and hell, that the church heartily and defiantly mocks these foes in Easter hymns such as this one by Paul Gerhardt:

Now hell, its prince, the devil,
Of all their pow'r are shorn;
Now I am safe from evil,
And sin I laugh to scorn.

Grim Death with all his might
Cannot my soul affright;
He is a pow'rless form,
Howe'er he rave and storm.

("Awake, My Heart, with Gladness," *TLH* 192:4)

So sings the church as they stand before the empty grave of Jesus, an everlasting emblem of our victory in Him.

Think back over the many trees and objects of wood you have studied: the trees in the Garden, the burning bush, the staff of Moses, the pole of the bronze serpent, the family tree of David, and now the cross. Discuss how they are related. How do they all convey a similar message about how God works in this world and in His church?

Conclusion

From the opening pages of the Bible to the end of Revelation, our Lord embraces His creation to such an extent that time and time again He takes even its most simple elements and uses them for extraordinary good. From the trees of Eden's Garden to the burning bush on Sinai, from the staff of Moses to the shoot of Jesse—all the way to the cross our heavenly Father uses trees and wood to bless His people. In, with, and under this wood—as well as nailed to it—is the God who works in ways unexpected by the world but welcomed and praised by the church. So we embrace the simplicity of this tree as our Lord embraced it. He embraced it with His Word, He filled it with His presence, and He painted it red with His own lifeblood. So we are not ashamed of it. The cross and crucifix in our churches are not closeted but held high, for with St. Paul we confess, "Far be it from me to boast except in the cross of our Lord Jesus Christ, by which the world has been crucified to me, and I to the world" (Galatians 6:14). So let us thank our God for the tree made sacred by His love, for in that tree is carved the epic of our salvation.

Closing Prayer

O sacred Head, now wounded,
With grief and shame weighed down,
Now scornfully surrounded
With thorns, Thine only crown.
O sacred Head, what glory,
What bliss, till now was Thine!
Yet, tho' despised and gory,
I joy to call Thee mine.

("O Sacred Head, Now Wounded," *TLH* 172:1)

THE TREE OF THE CROSS

Born to Die

How would you summarize, in one or two sentences, the message of Christmas? Which hymns in the Christmas season convey this same message?

Read aloud the stanzas from "What Child Is This" (*LW* 61). Compared to most other hymns about the nativity of our Lord, how is this hymn different? What coming event does it speak of? Why is this an important point for a hymn to make?

The Friday Called "Good"

In the vast majority of churches, there are far more people in church on Easter than on Good Friday. Why is that? What is it that keeps people from church on Good Friday but brings them on Easter? What are the implications of this inequality?

What is "good" about Good Friday? How would the world view this day? How does God view this day? As Jesus saw His cross approaching, how did He view it (**Hebrews 12:2**)? Can we rightly say that God was pleased to put His Son to death (**Isaiah 53:10**)? How can we say this?

On the Way to the Tree

Read Matthew **26:36–46**. What has already transpired on this night? Where are Jesus and the disciples now?

What does Paul say about Adam and Christ in **Romans 5:12–21**? In what ways are they alike and in what ways are they different?

Keeping in mind this corresponding relationship between the first Adam and the Second Adam, how is it significant that Jesus began His most intense sufferings in a garden (**Genesis 2:8–3:24**)?

Bearing the Wood

Read through the passion account of one of the four evangelists to see what happened after Jesus was arrested by the soldiers up until the moment He was led out to be crucified (**Matthew 26:57–27:26; Mark 14:53–15:20; Luke 22:54–23:25; John 18:12–19:16**).

Now read **Genesis 22:1–19** in light of the passion of our Lord. Note the parallels that exist between these two stories.

What connections are there between fathers and sons?

What geographical connection is there? Where was Mount Moriah, where Isaac was taken to be crucified? See **1 Chronicles 21:18–30; 2 Chronicles 3:1**.

How are both Isaac and Jesus of the seed of Abraham? (See **Genesis 12:7; 22:18; Galatians 3:16; KJV**.)

How were they both sons of promise?

Compare **Genesis 22:6** and **John 19:17**. What did both carry?

Yet how is the end of the story different for these two sons? In what way does the ram in **Genesis 22** foreshadow Jesus? How are we like Isaac (**Galatians 4:28**)?

The Place of the Skull

Jesus was crucified at a place called "Golgotha" in Aramaic; this is translated "the place of the skull." Although rooted in tradition and not in the Bible, the older explanation of this name says that Golgotha was so named because it was *the place of Adam's skull,* that is, his grave. Remember what you read in **Romans 5**. Also read **1 Corinthians 15:22**. Whether this tradition is true or not, how would the message it sends communicate the truth?

How might such a tradition also shed further light on Jesus' words to the repentant thief (**Luke 23:43**)?

The Crucified Serpent

Now that that passion account is fresh in your mind, recall what you studied in **Numbers 21** and **John 3:14** with regard to the bronze serpent. In what way is Jesus our "Serpent of salvation," as Luther called Him?

He Is Not Here

Read the account of our Lord's resurrection in one of the four Gospels. Why was it necessary for our Lord to be raised again (**Acts 2:24–31**)? How do we participate in both the crucifixion and the resurrection of Jesus (**Romans 6:1–11**)?

Think back over the many trees and objects of wood you have studied: the trees in the Garden, the burning bush, the staff of Moses, the pole of the bronze serpent, the family tree of David, and now the cross. Discuss how they are related. How do they all convey a similar message about how God works in His world and in His church?